A Little Give

Marina Benjamin's most recent books are *Insomnia*, *The Middlepause*, *Rocket Dreams*, shortlisted for the Eugene Emme Award, and *Last Days in Babylon*, longlisted for the Wingate Prize. Her writing has appeared in *Granta*, *The Guardian*, *The New York Times*, *New Philosopher*, and the digital magazines *Literary Hub* and *Aeon*, where she is a senior editor. She lives in London.

A Little Give

The Unsung, Unseen, Undone Work of Women

Marina Benjamin

SCRIBE

Melbourne • London

Scribe Publications
18–20 Edward St, Brunswick, Victoria 3056, Australia
2 John St, Clerkenwell, London, WC1N 2ES, United Kingdom
3754 Pleasant Ave, Suite 100, Minneapolis, Minnesota 55409, USA

Published by Scribe 2023

Typeset in Adoble Caslon Pro 8/10 pt by the publishers

Printed and bound in the UK by CPI Group (UK) Ltd,
Croydon CR0 4YY

Scribe Publications is committed to the sustainable use of natural
resources and the use of paper products made responsibly from
those resources.

978 1 957363 45 5 (US edition)
978 1 922585 66 0 (Australian edition)
978 1 914484 56 8 (UK edition)
978 1 922586 90 2 (ebook)

scribepublications.com
scribepublications.com.au
scribepublications.co.uk

For the cleaners and the carers

When we speak of housework we are not speaking of a job as other jobs, but we are speaking of the most pervasive manipulation, the most subtle and mystified violence that capitalism has ever perpetrated against any section of the working class.

Silvia Federici, Wages Against Housework

There are those who want 'only the best' and those who believe only-the-best is immoral. I would talk about these two impulses, one for comfort, the other for justice, and how one appears animal, the other not that animal at all …

Anne Boyer, Garments Against Women

Content(ion)s

Cleaning   1

Pleasing   33

Feeding   69

Caring   99

Safeguarding   131

Lapsing   167

Launching   185

Acknowledgements   217

Notes   221

Cleaning

The sharp-sweet hit of ammonia is unmistakable. It prickles the nostrils like something administered for a faint and once I detect it I smell it everywhere. Urine, gone stale.

Standing at the kitchen sink, arms deep in dirty dishes, I twist my head away from the most obvious offender, a dirty grey dishcloth balled up behind the faucet. But now stinging fumes of ammonia are rising up from every surface like swamp mist. Everything is suspect. The grimed-up lino flooring, the rag-headed mop propped against the back door, the stiffened mat beneath my feet. My aunt, I realise, is incontinent.

Beyond the kitchen window the plum tree at the end of the garden is in bud. I think about the jam G would make if we were to return at the end of summer and gather up an overripe cache in juice-stained paper bags. I picture him at the stove stirring bubbling goo, purple on the wooden spoon, filling the house with wafts of boiled fruit. In years gone by aunt Marta would have brought the plums round herself, along with a variety of cottonwool-swaddled plant cuttings that she'd instruct us to graft into our small city garden. But Marta hasn't left the house in almost two years.

Next door in the living room my mother sits with her, muttering quietly, the conversation a one-way affair. Every now and then she strokes her sister's impassive hand. It used to be that Marta was the big personality, blowing into our house like a tempest, trailing cigarette smoke, regaling us with her latest triumphs and derelictions — upbraiding an errant neighbour, tearing up a parking ticket right in front of the idiot meter man — her eyes alive with mischief. The raw energy she brought with her! Its bee-sting brace. But my aunt has been mute for months.

I lean back from the sink and hold my yellow gloves aloft, dripping soap suds, to peer through the small rectangular hatch with sliding plastic panes that connects the two rooms, and I see them there: my aunt ensconced in her faded orange armchair, slippered feet planted stolidly in front of her, my mother on the sofa next to her. Their knees are touching and this moves me in a way I find hard to articulate. There's something about the cargo of the shared past they carry between them that's impressed within this physical contact, a bond so intense it's almost twinship.

For a brief moment I picture them as they once were, young women impatient for their lives to begin, eager to know what lay ahead. Dressed in white shirts and full skirts, tightly belted at the waist in the 1950s style, they're leaning over the railing of the ocean liner that would sweep them away from Jewish Baghdad forever, faces turned to the wind; my mother a gamine creature with a flick of black hair falling over her shy eyes, Marta altogether more va-va-voom, her Rita Hayworth curls squashed by the smartly frogged ship's officer's cap that she'd snagged within minutes of boarding and wore at a tilt.

I cannot catch any of my mother's words, just their sound, like water slipping over stones, but Marta regards her with adoring, child-wide eyes and for a flickering moment I am convinced that recognition is still there. But if it is, it is trapped inside a brain too demented to return anything. What I'm surveying resembles a still-life painting. The projection of intimacy is all my own.

In three hours' time I am meant to be at the National Theatre. I could walk away from this suburban kitchen right now and my aunt would be none the wiser. But the drag I feel in my bones tells me that walking away is not an option. I feel the need to honour her, to offer some tribute to her personhood before it is completely eroded by brain-rot: to restore, if not exactly her dignity, then at least some version of order. By way of erecting a symbolic shrine, built of formica and lino and corrugated plastic, and dedicating it to the woman she once was. I will make her kitchen gleam.

Opening cupboards one by one I find the tools I need:

bleach, floor cleaner, J-cloths, paper towels, anti-mould spray, window cleaner, lime de-scaler, wipes, scrubbing sponges. (I will not be using the rag-headed mop.) And I begin. This is devotional work, executed out of love and filial duty, appreciation and grief. Payback for the care my aunt showered on me growing up: jumping in to take my side in my endless altercations with my mother; driving me home across London at manic speeds on nights when I'd changed my mind about sleeping over, a fag in her mouth, her shoulders hunched over the steering wheel in concentration. She was always carrying sweets, always conspiratorial, always up for some childish fun.

As I clean I feel my heart lighten. Scraping caked-on food off the counter, spritzing windows and taps, the sticky hob, the nicotine-stained cupboard doors. Grabbing a bin bag I waltz it open and fill it with food gone bad in the fridge. I get the worst of the sticky grime off the floor with boiling water and bleach, then I dowse a fat sponge with liquid cleaner and adopt a strange half-squat that lets me take large arcing sweeps at the floor without having to get down on my knees. I push aside niggling thoughts of Marta idly surveying me, waving a lazy hand and saying *why bother?* A reluctant cook, indifferent to dirt, her kitchen was never clean. And yet my urge is to pick up after her, brush away the scattered pieces, tidy any evidence that might betray her broken mind.

An hour later the kitchen is transformed. It even smells clean. So why do I feel soiled, as though dirt, degradation and dementia were somehow catching?

I want to leave a physical marker, a totem of shiny pots and pans, a cairn. I want to bequeath a commemorative gift that says 'care has been lavished here'. This is why people set vases of fresh-cut flowers on the kitchen table. It's an invitation to pause and smell the air, to understand that something good lives in this atmosphere. But there are no flowers here, only a row of forlorn-looking cacti on the shelf under the window, wobbly in their powdery earth. I water them, as if spilling blood.

Next door my mother is saying, 'We need to head home now, Marta, but I'll call you tomorrow'. And 'don't worry, we'll be back in a couple of weeks'. She says: 'You have Elise to look after you in the meantime'.

Elise is a Montenegrin woman of statuesque proportions and hypermobile expressiveness. She lives in Ashford with her two teenage sons and drives up to Shepperton every day to cook for Marta. Arriving as we are readying to leave she bustles in carrying plastic bags and Tupperware containers. She towers over us, bestowing greetings and hugs, her features beaming.

'Hello darling', she calls out to Marta from the hall before heading to the kitchen to unpack soup and bread and Fig Newtons.

She will stay all afternoon, make Marta an evening meal, read aloud to her a dozen or so pages from a history book or detective novel, and watch TV, talking back to the newscasters while Marta sits silently by. Then she'll help

Marta up to her narrow bed and turn out the lights. Until the next day.

'Oh my God, a fairy has come and made magic', Elise says, as she walks into the shining kitchen, putting a thick hand to her eyes as if to shield them from the unexpected glare.

It's a clever thing to say. She means that I have not abased myself by doing menial work, work that she understands to be beneath me — and also beneath her, since she never stoops to do it, the line between cleaner and carer being a defining demarcation. Instead my work is fairy dust and glitter; a wand waved rather than a demeaning labour. I am a benevolent sprite.

At the theatre — running, I manage to claim my seat moments before the curtain rises — I am agitated. I am convinced that I stink of wee. My daily life and Marta's spool out across parallel worlds, the distance between them never more palpable than in this instant when our differences are so rudely exposed, and the breach has left me discomfited. The play is about vigilantes organising under the negligent eye of a corrupt leadership in Pakistan in the early 1980s, seeding what would soon become the Taliban. In the interval I sip wine with G and a friend and talk politics, and feel my grip on my own life returning.

As we talk, the fumes of ammonia, detergent and bleach gradually lift and dissipate into my surrounds. My agitation is diluted. I am one part in a million. A speck of dust.

In a single moment I see myself as others might see me, a dogged woman squatting on the kitchen floor, skirt hitched up around her thighs, head pressed forward, one hand splayed on the tiles for balance. The other hand, the left, is making determined circular passes across one of the tiles, scrubbing it clean with a baby wipe.

In this moment I exist on multiple planes. I see myself from the outside and I think: this is madness, this crazed cleaning of an already-clean floor. I think that a middle-aged woman on her knees in the kitchen has lost the plot, or lost herself, or is lost in a task of such meaninglessness that it must offer some meditative balm. Inside my head thoughts flutter about, come to rest for a second and assume definite shape, then flutter off again.

'All the work of the hand is rooted in thinking', Heidegger wrote. 'The hand does not only grasp and catch, or push and pull. The hand reaches and extends, receives and welcomes ... The hand carries. The hand designs and signs ...'

Heidegger was talking about handiwork, the dignity of making things. He was talking about an artisanship rooted in skill and learning. Cleaning does not qualify: it is mindless work. In cleaning even the hand is dumb. Down on the floor in the kitchen I think only lowly thoughts. I think: look at this tile, strafed with solvent so powerful it can remove gloss paint from slate. I consider the wipe in my hand and I think: this solvent is so potent, imagine what it could do to a baby's bottom.

1

Housework is an activity that erases itself. By that I do not mean that it is undone because it is in the entropic nature of things to tend towards chaos — although that too is true. I mean that the success of housework turns on its invisibility, on the quiet conspiracy of the women who do it and then hide the fact of its doing, denying the physicality of their own labour.

2

In grand Victorian households the servant women who were paid to do housework were supposed to be invisible. Concealed behind the walls, they moved through the many-storeyed houses they upkept using a labyrinth of back passages, narrow corridors and separate stairways, ferrying clean piles of linens and gleaming soup tureens from one room to another in the company of spiders and rodents.

By night they melted into the air, disappearing into unloved attics.

3

Sometimes the hidden is fetishised.

The Swedish-Italian artist Linda Fregni Nagler works with anonymous found photographs dating from the 19th century and assembles them into meaningful archives. Her book *The Hidden Mother* (2013) contains more than 1,000 studio-made portrait pictures of infants, in which

the mother's presence (a functional necessity
to hold the babies still during long exposure
times) has been crudely obliterated. Either
a blanket has been thrown over her body
or her head is bandaged up inside a scarf
or she's squatting unseen behind a chair.
Sometimes only a supporting hand is visible.
In other pictures the negative was scratched
or burned to leave a blackened gouge where
the mother's head should be. The images are
uncanny, violent, disturbing.

Perhaps the intent is to foreground the
child, in keeping with an ethos that rewards
wives and mothers for producing clean
houses and washed children without ever
taking credit for them. The mothers must
stay in the background, unseen.

However, not seeing these mothers relies
on the viewer wilfully ignoring the cloth-
covered lump in the middle of the frame.
We find the photos uncanny not because
they are alien but because the dynamic they
make visible is uncomfortably familiar.

What the images tell me is that oppression
and privilege can sit alongside one another,

that no matter the class standing these
women might enjoy, the primary taint
of womanhood — demanding erasure
— prevails.

4

The American sitcom *Bewitched* was
a weekly staple on British TV screens
when I was growing up in the 1970s. Its
comedy relied on viewers knowing that the
show's lead character, Samantha Stephens,
played by a wholesome and enviably
blond Elizabeth Montgomery, was not the
suburban housewife she appeared to be,
but a white witch equipped with magical
powers. Samantha could cast spells on
people in the manner of a mesmerist. With
a click of her fingers she would teleport
from place to place and when she twitched
her nose like a rabbit material objects
magically reordered themselves.

Every evening before her husband, Darrin,
returned home from the office Samantha
would do the cute thing with her nose and
her messy house would instantly transform

from rubbish tip to conjugal temple. Then she'd throw herself onto the sofa, set her feet upon the coffee table and peruse a magazine as if she hadn't a care in the world. Thus would Darrin find her, believing she had spent the whole day merely waiting for him.

Bewitched was riddled with subtext. It is one reason the show continues to have an afterlife in the pages of feminist journals. On the surface it seemed to be arguing that the production of a fine-looking house and not the work that went into staging it was any housewife's acknowledged achievement. In other words, that all housework has to be magically executed. But the message tugging uncomfortably at the viewer's sleeve underscored that a powerful woman must pretend that her powers do not exist so as never to show up a man who cannot countenance them.

The marriage at the heart of *Bewitched* was built on a silent pact between Darrin and Samantha. The deal was this: he loved her *in spite of* her powers, while her side of the bargain was to do her utmost to disown them. The trouble was she couldn't help herself. She was always cheating: after all what woman faced with the tedious reality of household chores wouldn't take a short cut?

A gratifying footnote to the series' portrayal of domestic bliss is that in real life Elizabeth Montgomery was a vocal campaigner for women's rights and also a champion of gay rights — often in tandem with Dick Sargent, the second actor to play Darrin in the show, who later came out as gay.

I do not enjoy this work.

I am not one of those women who buys the line
that housework is a Zen activity
a doorway into contemplative absence
a means of zoning out.
Whenever I get obsessive about it,
which I do, I feel as if I am reverting
to type. My mother's type.
The type of woman valued by patriarchy.

An economy of care is in play here
— though not everyone is a player.
It does not feature on the stock market
or have any recognised public value
yet care can be bought and sold

and traded to a third party.
Who receives care, who offers it?
And at what price?
These are vital questions for any woman.

Let us not delude ourselves,
housework is not a skill
but a service. There is little expertise involved,
only brute labour — which is cheap.
Housework is not generative.
It is rather a work of maintenance
and it never ends:
every week, it needs to be done anew.

It took me years to hire someone to clean my house.
My mess was mine to clear away.
In housework our everyday life and our possessions
are laid bare;
under the attentive eyes of another I feel exposed.
Everything I own turned to underwear.

What does Carlotta make of me
when all she has to go on is what I own
— and what I can pay?
In front of her I am ashamed of my plenty.
I do a pre-clean before she comes.

When Carlotta is around I feel compelled to work,

justifying my entitlement to her labour.
I tap uncomfortably at my laptop.
But all I am really signalling
is that my work is worth more than her work.

The funny thing is
Carlotta finally appeared to relax around me
on a day I was too sick to work.
I curled up on the sofa in my pyjamas
to watch crap daytime TV.
Carlotta loved it.
At last, I was behaving in a way that made sense.
I was doing what she would like to do
if she wasn't mopping my floors.

It wasn't parsimony that made me suggest
she clean fortnightly instead of weekly,
but guilt.
I ought to have inquired if her preference
was to rest her bones
or earn more.

My mother herself did not work, at least not outside of the house, and within the house she availed herself of hired help. Josefina, or Fina for short, was her cleaning lady when I was growing up. A Spaniard from the north of the country Fina had pale, thin skin, crinkle-rimmed round her eyes, and coal-black hair the texture of twigs. Stiff strands were forever escaping the hairpins she used to pin it away from her face. Between dusting and hoovering and cleaning the floor on her hands and knees Fina liked to dance, and when she danced, Flamenco-style, her fleshy upper arms wobbled.

My friends and I used to egg her on, clapping and laughing as she stamped and twirled. In the way that children are cruel we thought the joke was on her, but I see now that it was she who humoured us.

Fina's wardrobe consisted entirely of clinging

polyester, the cheap kind that was patterned with colourful swirls and smelled of stale sweat. Whenever she danced the room would take on an almost feral scent. When Fina arrived at our house in the summer she'd exchange her outdoor shoes for low-wedged mules, exposing cracked skin along the sides of the soles of her feet and on her heels. In winter she wore thick nylon tights that bunched up her toes. Tucked away at home, out of sight of the clients she cleaned for, was a layabout husband who did not work. Fina used to complain that he was a good for nothing, always loafing.

Judging from the black eyes she'd sometimes be sporting when she arrived she must have given him the occasional mouthful. Then again maybe he was just a bad-tempered drunk. Maybe he didn't need excuses or provocations. Maybe he just hit her to make himself feel better. The truth is I knew nothing of Fina's inner life or the complex reality of her relationships. Only that on black-eye days there was no dancing.

I met her sons a few times because she'd bring them over during the school holidays and they'd watch TV while she cleaned, surly and silent. They were named Carlos and Juan. Carlos was squat and broody and grew up to hit his mother, just like his dad did. I don't know what happened to Juan, who sat on the sofa and snarled, 'What are you looking at?' But I hope he escaped.

Poor Fina. She looked a decade older than her 50-odd years. Yet before her age caught up to the way she looked she was dead. Felled by exhaustion, neglect, and most likely misery. 'She had a hard life', sighs my mother, every time she mentions her.

Fina's life was oppressed, distorted and most likely curtailed by patriarchy, class and capitalism. I wonder if my mother, now 90 and struggling to find meaning in her own longevity, feels anything like remorse over engaging Fina to do hard manual work, and contributing, however unwittingly, to her early demise. Like it or not, my mother was party to the forces that oppressed her. Yet by paying Fina my mother also gave her a measure of independence — admittedly not enough to free her from a brutal (and likely brutalised) man, but perhaps this gets to the heart of a central feminist contradiction about how we talk and think about labour in the home: we understand its necessity yet its punishing nature and demeaning connotations feel inescapable, part of the currency of our shared understanding. It's why actually getting 'wages for housework'— to literalise the 1970s' most brazen political campaign — will never liberate women.

As I near the age Fina was when she died I begin to understand the real physical toll exacted by domestic work. I'd like to let Fina know that I haven't the heart for it anymore, either. Hauling the vacuum cleaner up the stairs has become a labour in itself; getting down on my knees is an impulse I need to check. Pushing my body in these ways elicits protest, strange clicking sounds, mysterious spasms of pain, general aches and stiffness.

The satisfaction that I derive from serving another, that can make of housework a gift, as it was in Marta's kitchen, is wholly lacking in my own domain, where cleaning has become an ordeal and also a double-bind: because whenever my clean house comes courtesy of Carlotta my self-care can only be purchased through her work.

I use the term self-care fully aware of its popular association with luxury and frivolity, expensive skin products and day spas, as if diving into a bubble bath to shut out the world at the end of a hard day were an act of defiance. Yet the true meaning of self-care is bound up with feminist activism, the idea being that by caring for yourself you are better able to care for others, showing up when they need you and donating your time and energy to organising for community causes and activist resistance. This is self-care, as Audre Lorde described it in *A Burst of Light*, not as 'self-indulgence' but 'self-preservation'. It is 'an act of political warfare' by which Black women in particular might rescue themselves from 'the devastating effects of overextension'.

Lorde saw self-care as a means of escaping a hidden economy, an underground capitalism that drives women to make unacceptable trades, weighing the value of their waged labour against their ability to participate in more meaningful work.

But if hiring Carlotta to clean my house is a necessary act of self-care, saving my midlife body from the ardours of physical labour while freeing me to undertake ('higher status', according to patriarchy) 'white-collar' work, does it not also make me part of the oppressive economy that underfunds feminised labour? Does it not leave me compromised?

That it is largely women alone who are forced to grapple with these questions is yet another aspect of patriarchy. Men don't even ask themselves these questions: they just hire people to clean for them and get on with their lives.

I don't like to examine my mother's relationship with Fina too closely because I know that my mother was not sufficiently exercised by its fundamental inequalities. Their relationship was hierarchical, transactional, the loyalty all on one side. It was exclusively driven by my mother's expectations. She made it known that she had 'standards' and was insensible to the fact that these were often unreasonable. She resented Fina taking a coffee break on her dime and complained if the crystal drops hanging off the living-room chandelier weren't dusted perfectly; Fina's work was never as good a job as she would have made of it were she minded to attempt it, which she was not. She never sent Fina home either, when she showed up with a black eye, never pressed a few notes into her hand, telling her not to bother with the cleaning. She'd just pretend the black eye wasn't there.

My mother is not a heartless woman: around people she loves she is putty, marshmallow, mush. What she lacks are management skills. Aside from a one-time encounter with the working world, when Air France employed her as a 'ground hostess' in the late 1950s and early 1960s — an era that saw her subject to regular bottom pinching — she has never been party to office politics. She has never had to manage someone else's workload (as opposed to directing their labour) or accommodate their commitments and complaints. She was raised in a culture in which women of her class never worked, their social status being uniquely pinned to how well they ran their households. My mother is highly competent, but the only power she has ever known is the one patriarchy invests in housewifery, the better to keep women in their place. My mother is not heartless. But she is guilty of collusion.

At a deeper level I suspect my mother lacked empathy for Fina because Fina stood for every aspect of femininity she wished to escape. Like my mother Fina was an immigrant, but a 'bad' one, someone without means or status, who was unable to contribute to society and whose labours were servile not productive. Fina drew from people a response my mother feared attracting to herself, namely pity — 'Poor Fina'. Yet my mother was also trapped by patriarchy. It's so strange how women are sometimes harshest in judging other women, precisely because we cannot abide to acknowledge our vulnerability as shared.

I wonder where all this places me. Fina was my first exposure to positionality. From her presence in our lives I learnt that housework is political, a trade-off between freedom and labour, privilege and need. Nor, in years since, have I made a better job of this commerce. In outsourcing my domestic work to buy myself time to spend as I choose I am not so different from my mother, even if I recognise my part in oppressing another woman.

I still do more housework than I want to — and much more of it than G, who takes on a good deal more housework than most men. Literally as I write I can hear him vacuuming the stairs. He takes the bins out every week, clears our blocked drains of organic slime and gunk. Even so housework is not ingrained into the fibre of his being as it is with me. Dirt doesn't get under his skin. There is no ledger lodged in G's brain that tells him exactly what is and isn't in the fridge, when the bedsheets were last changed or if the carpet's due for anti-moth treatment. He rarely tackles the skirting boards or washes down the woodwork with sugar soap. Cobwebs and dust devils do not cast a shadow over his days.

It would never occur to G to think that by hiring someone else to clean for us his place in the world might be compromised.

I wish I could tell you that domestic work is something I am able to parcel across my days like any other commitment slotted into my schedule. But it isn't like that. It isn't a displacement activity or sublimation, consuming me because I cannot face up to something else, or an innocent distraction that allows me to do thinking work while my hands digress. For me the impulse to clean mimics the way I succumb to infection: when the viral load is small the urge to do it is a continual low-level thrum, something motivating, like a back-of-the-mind niggle with little compulsive affect. But when the viral load is great I fall sick for cleaning.

Over time I have come to believe that domestic care is a labour unlike any other. Whether it involves lowly housework, the mopping up of a loved one's pee or attending to the needs of the hired help whose job is to clean for you (helping Carlotta fill out her tax forms; beefing up her job applications to work as a school cook) it entails a kind of emotional washing up. It involves submitting to a rinse cycle that dislodges the ego, leaving only finer feelings.

Perhaps such finer feelings are the reward of someone who spreads themselves so thin that everything about them is finer — practically translucent, filmy and insubstantial. This is a dangerous kind of delicacy it seems to me and yet this is where caring can take us, away from our centres and out to the edges, stretched so thin (and wound so tight) we risk losing ourselves.

All it takes is a split second's inattention. I'll fixate on a few stray pubic hairs curled on the bathroom tiles and something in my blood stirs. Down on my knees, bone-awkward on tile, I root out the body's offending slough, scrub at every dubious biological smear. I think: these tiles are new enough to have no business reflecting back anything but sparkle. I think that when I'm done with this floor you'll be able to eat off it.

I picture the ghost-self of my mother playing my DNA like guitar strings. I think: I'm too old to be doing this. Also: I've got better things to do with my time. But I do not get up from the floor until I am done. Until all the spindly little spiders parasailing off the skirting boards have pulled up rope and run away to hide.

Let me be clear, I am not enjoying myself. Though after a fashion — a bygone fashion, a patriarchal fashion

— I do feel self-satisfied. I tell myself that Carlotta would never go hammer and tongs at this. Not the way I do.

Marta dies in her own bed, as she wanted. We get the call from Elise in the morning and are there by lunchtime. Elise is inconsolable. Upstairs, with hazy light coming through the smudged bedroom window in biblical shafts, Marta at first looks to be asleep, her body gently curled towards the wall, her eyes closed. But without breath to animate her she seems suspended, as if a moment's pause has been theatrically drawn out. Her mouth is open, her cheeks sunken, a few threadbare strands of wispy white hair fluff up at the crown of her head. Her stillness is absolute. This is the first dead body I have ever encountered and it looks as if it has been evacuated. Left behind. I wonder if turning to face the wall was her last intentional act.

I do due diligence, which is another, more bureaucratic kind of care. I visit the local registry office to get a death certificate, call the GP, alert the synagogue that holds Marta's burial plan, and whose duty staff send a hearse to collect her body later that afternoon. Jewish law decrees that a body must be buried within 24 hours. You haven't time to think about anything until your loved one is already underground. Gone.

A couple of weeks later, when my mother is better able to face things, we return to Marta's empty house to execute a clean-up. This is a different kind of domestic labour, not a job of weekly maintenance but a once-and-for-all erasure of everything that was. A second funeral.

Many of Marta's possessions will go to the rag-and-bone, much of it to landfill. We sort through cupboards full of mothballed clothing and shoes that smell of dry earth and stone. We tackle drawers stuffed with pale manila folders, each of them bulging with administrative guff: bills, banks statements, corporate flyers, long-expired insurance policies. So much rubbish to measure a life by. As we work, sneezing occasionally amid the tomb-like layers of dust we've stirred, I think of Anne Carson asking, what's dirty? And answering: sex, secrets, clothes.

We book a skip.

There is surprisingly little to salvage. I find a tea set that looks as though it has never been used, possibly from the 1970s, possibly Japanese made, its swirly glaze and fiery colours reminding me of Marta's unruliness. I fish out a thick foolscap photograph album from the TV trolley, full of large black-and-white pictures of Marta's early travels in Europe with her new husband, Victor. Page by page I glimpse a Marta I never knew, kitted out in boxy Jackie Kennedy suits, her bobbed hair curling up at the ends. And there is Victor in his dark baggy suits, insisting on wearing a tie in the midday heat. He has craggy good looks, though he's already running to fat. Both of them are smoking in every picture — at the Acropolis, in Parisian cafés, on the Spanish Steps in Rome. The pictures date from their honeymoon, before they set up home together in Tehran in the 1960s; a smart young couple with everything ahead of them, unaware that Victor would die tragically young.

For Marta nothing that followed could equal those early years with Victor by her side. After he died she turned their house into a museum that commemorated their lives together: she wouldn't countenance changing a thing and this suited her since it became an ambition of hers to exist as an artefact exists, rooted in the past.

My aunt never cleaned and she almost never cooked. She always maintained that she couldn't see the point. She never 'entertained' either, as my mother called it — the term perfectly capturing how, for her, socialising was not about having friends over and breaking bread with them, but was instead a kind of strained high-wire act: another duty to perform, like cleaning. A duty Marta refused. Yet she was the life and soul of any gathering she graced, chain-smoking, telling her funny stories, laughing her gurgling laugh, generous with her love.

If I had to sum up Marta in a single word I'd say she was indolent. She wanted life to be lived at a languid pace, preferred haze to focus, reverie to reality. She lived out her days marking time with the lighting of each cigarette, counting down every individual breath she would take until she next met Victor.

All the while the dust in her house kept piling. By the time she died, that dust was so thick as to have acquired substance. It was furry as moss. Sticky like honey. Coating everything, finding every tiny nook to settle in and clogging the air at the least sign of movement, it remained stubbornly visible. The thick dust of indolence, of failing to entertain, of refusing to be spread thin. It was Marta's last triumph.

Pleasing

When I was small my father used to summon me to the bathroom of a morning and make sure I was fit to be seen. He'd cup my face in the soft-padded palm of his hand, tilt my chin up so that my face caught the light and scrutinise my features. He'd look for sleep crusts in my eyes that needed rinsing out. Scan for remnants of just-eaten breakfast between my crooked teeth. Then he'd dab a finger on his tongue to wet it before smoothing my brows into neat arcs. He took his own sweet time with this ritual, releasing me only when he was satisfied I looked 'presentable'.

I remember then having to race around getting my school things together while my mother waited impatiently by the front door, chastising my father for delaying me with his nonsense and fretting over her wristwatch. No sooner was I by her side than she'd whisk us out of the house, speeding along the back streets of our neighbourhood in her sky-blue Cortina.

They had different energies, my parents. And different aptitudes.

My father couldn't drive. While my mother motored around, seeing to her daily chores, stopping off at the supermarket before picking up fabric samples from dad's suppliers, he would idle in bed, emerging — ideally — only once we were safely out from under his feet to breakfast in his pyjamas in peace. Maybe he'd thumb through the pages of the *Drapers Record* as he ate: oats sprinkled with watermelon seeds and soaked in enough milk to turn everything to soup. Or he'd be dreaming up garments to sew for a precious new client into whom he poured his hopes of propping up his flagging couture business. Either way it was understood that my father needed quiet in the morning. Too much noise and activity sent him into a tizz.

I understood other things as well. Knew my father wasn't capable the way my mother was. That he was lucky to have her fix his meals and manage his accounts. That she, not he, was the boss: he did what he was told to do, by her, at his own sluggish pace. I also knew that he was creative and, with it, volatile.

Over time he'd perfected the art of absenting himself from the family circle even when he was manifestly there — like so many other men who disappear into offices, dens or sheds and think manly thoughts. Often he'd retreat behind shut doors to take long afternoon naps or seek refuge in the bathroom for hours on end. I've no idea what he did in there, only that he would exit in a cloud of steam as if from a Norwegian sauna, a towel neatly wrapped round his soft middle, his large green eyes bulging like a sea monster's. After showering for what seemed like an eternity and draining the boiler of hot water he must have busied himself tweezing, talcing and preening — trying to tame the stubborn kink out of his black hair — before he surfaced red-faced and smelling like a flower, the curled dark hairs on his chest still glistening with damp.

In the evenings he would slip out of the house in his long wool coat and polished brogues, a haze of Aramis aftershave lingering in his wake, not to be glimpsed again until the early hours.

Sometimes I'd wake in the middle of the night and hear raised voices downstairs, my mother giving him grief him for losing money at one of London's smarter casinos. When she demanded that he hand over his cash he'd clown-frown and turn out his empty trouser pockets to show her he hadn't a sou, like a bad vaudeville character.

My father was a night wanderer, keeping hours different from the rest of us, rejoicing in the nocturnal life — the green baize of lamplit gaming tables, the twinkling glamour of evening wear, dark rain slicking empty streets. Looking back I see that his powerful need for private space in the midst of family life was constitutional in other ways. It protected his solitary sense of himself as an artist and bolstered his dreamy perception of being a player in a glossy world of money and entitlement that, in reality, he could only touch at the hemlines. He always believed he was born for better things, even as life repeatedly told him otherwise.

It was my father who taught me how to be a woman. My mother, officious, controlling and goal-driven, effectively gave herself up to busywork, yanking her housewife's agenda into the public sphere as far as it would go without pulling out its gendered roots, while he concerned himself with my cultural entrainment, purporting to know exactly what a woman ought to show the world and what to hide, what she might hope for and what lay beyond her ken.

He used to beckon me to sit beside him on the sofa and together we'd flip through back issues of *Paris Match* while he passed judgement on the movie stars and socialites splashed across its pages. Growing voluble and excited he'd pronounce this one too dumpy to wear stripes and that one too doll-like, her waxy-looking gown a tasteless confection of flounces and puffs. 'Look at her', he'd tell me, pointing to some glamorous young starlet: 'she doesn't have the chest to carry off a décolletage'.

He, not my mother, selected my clothes. Frilly dresses in floral prints that embarrassed me in front of my pre-teen peers. A toothy, bony child, painfully self-conscious at being kitted out in barrettes and bows, I would lurk in corners at birthday parties, watching other girls titter at me from across the room, their hands clamped to their mouths to dramatise their scorn.

My father's faith in the transformative magic of clothing was boundless. After studying couture in postwar Paris in a many-windowed building that had once been a ballet school he interned at Maison Dior, becoming a devotee of the New Look and sticking with it long after its popularity faded. Famed for its flagrant anti-austerity aesthetic the New Look was defined by its full-skirted excesses and its retrograde femininity: hip-padded, wasp-waisted, pointy-breasted. Coco Chanel, her lean, androgynous clothing the very antithesis to Dior's feminine mystique, once quipped that Dior didn't so much dress women as upholster them.

My father didn't get on with Chanel. The clean lines she favoured over curves, her playful samplings of masculine tweeds, her love of black and white, her practical-looking hats. In dressing forward-thinking women she had, in his view, created an army of cross-dressers as militant in the social freedoms they claimed as she had famously been. He disapproved.

The costuming of women was something we lived and breathed at home. My mother's cupboards were bursting with exuberant one-off creations — a palette of pastels hand-stitched by my father. Bolts of fabric lay about everywhere, propped against walls; boxes of beads, ribbons, felts and pebble-shaped ironing pads filled unclaimed drawers. Most evenings after supper my parents converted our breakfast room into a pin-strewn hive of industry, transforming it into an outpost of my father's West End showrooms.

For me the very image of home is the picture of my parents sitting at the formica-topped rectangular table, vexing sheer chiffon or faille creations under the half-light of the day's end. Delicate dresses in various states of deconstruction occupy the surfaces around them and the steam iron is on permanent stand-by, furzing the air with its heavy breathing. Above the measuring and tacking and marking up my mother and father keep up a constant chatter, gossiping about high society and debating the various balls and banquets to which these dresses, like liquid *laissez-passers*, would afford them entry.

I remember thinking at the time how unreal, how slippery, their innocent speculations seemed. Not because the upper crust wasn't as hedonistic as ever, but because I didn't think my Iraqi-Jewish parents could have any part of it. Somewhere in their logic I sensed a category mistake. Though my father could never admit as much, his clients saw him as a tradesman and not, as he believed, a friend. Inoculated by glamour my parents were oblivious to the contrast between their vivid daydreaming and the uniform grey-brown palette of outer London suburbia that spread beyond their window. Yet they were never closer as a couple than when they were sitting at that table making clothes together. For once they were a united front.

In the summer of 1979 I turned 15. I had begun to stretch, acceding to the pull of a world beyond that of my parents. Hungry to find myself, it seemed as if I'd spent my entire life on some lonely floating island, cut off from the greater landmass of culture and civilisation. Consumed with the need to escape — my every other teenage desire dwarfed by it — those formative years narrowed to a quest for ways and means.

Once I turned a forensic eye on my own upbringing it was like wearing X-ray specs. There were so many things I didn't just see, but saw through. I saw that all my bearings were skewed towards the East. Picked up on how my migrant parents, having failed entirely to find in England anything they recognised as home, protected themselves from psychic rupture by pretending nothing in their orbit had changed.

All around me were crowded cultural touchstones that shored up their illusion. Aromatic rice dishes that infused our house with notes of saffron and cumin; a guttural language slanted with dialect and brimming in equal parts with hospitality and invective and which I, caught between two worlds, understood but could not speak. There were drawers full of amulets to ward off the evil eye, and the ever-present press of extended family, gossiping and eating (always eating) and singing wailing songs, like dirges, that gave voice to the timeworn values we lived by. Everything familiar took on the appearance of a semaphore, packing what I now regarded as coercive meaning into innocent outwards signs.

At some level I'd always grasped my outsider status. At school I kept company with the rest of the misfits, children held close to strange tongues and stranger palates. Hiromi Miyamoto, with her cherry blossom–print satchel and enviably miniature pencil sets, and Raka Prakash, who hid her regal face behind a slick of black hair, each of us robbed of the power to define herself on her native terrain. We answered instead to taunts of 'you're foreign', masking the wound of it beneath playground pluck, that particular f-word still summing up for me the incurious racism of 1970s Britain, transmitted from parents to children as if — like the amulets my family kissed or hid in their clothing — it offered some kind of protective charm. Inside the chalk circle everyone belongs, but mind the outside where foreign bodies roam.

Taking charge of my own othering I turned my back on everything my family upheld — seemingly imported from medieval Iraq — starting with their clannish conservatism, their concern with face and their attachment to shame, and I staked my claim on the forbidden world.

Mine was a most conventional rebellion except that

in the world I came from the stakes were higher. I took up Benson & Hedges cigarettes, heavy on the tar, and persevered with them. Filled the empty hours of boredom and yearning lying on my bedroom floor and blasting out brain-jangling punk on my clunky cassette player. Styled myself a clever-clogs, as beholden to facts as my father was to fancies. Burning with teenage indignation, I signed up to far-left ideologies, confidently holding forth on the merits of Soviet-style communism without the least understanding of its lived experience.

But in spite of my new-found power to generate convulsions in family life I remained desperate for my parents' approval.

I had been programmed well. My childhood home was a factory of femininity. A site of cultural reproduction. It had been drummed into my core that women were put on this planet to please. As my mother so well exemplified they should support their menfolk, push them forward and have their backs, swallowing their own anger and aspirations in order to be the glue that bonds families together. They should be easy on the eye too, shoving under the glossy cover of their exterior bodywork all the effort it took to get there.

Though I was not so naïve as to believe that I could change their values I wanted my parents to acknowledge that my right to self-definition was as legitimate as theirs. The principle of the thing mattered because it gave me unarguable grounds for turning decisively from the pathways Iraqi-Jewish culture laid out before me — their common destination, early marriage, man-pleasing and, as I saw it, spiritual death.

I had seen how women in my family and its circle deferred to fathers, uncles, husbands; how they aspired to be model homemakers and mothers and then internalised the psychological cost, and I wanted no part of it. No one expected women to be brainless, but the compromises demanded of them were in some ways worse: ideally, Iraqi-Jewish culture desired women to be crafty enough to outwit other women, yet never so clever as to show up a man. Almost any kind of female ambition was frowned upon. In my parent's moral universe only teaching and the medical arts, those classically portable Jewish professions, and caring professions were above suspicion.

With a kind of inchoate longing I recognised that a handful of my peers were raised by working mothers — modern professionals with strident, free-thinking ways, and, more often than not, divorced — who seemed to me exotic creatures whose bright plumage and winged sorties into the wider world spoke to a way of living I could not begin to fathom. I remember one mother in particular who wore ribbed, poloneck sweaters, short skirts and knee-high suede boots. Never home when I visited after school she'd breeze in as I was leaving, the smell of the city, of grime and money, confidence and fulfilment, clinging to her skin and making it glow.

If someone had told me that in time I'd be more like

her than my own mother I'd never have believed them. Though a sixth sense also told me that if I did chase freedom there would be penalties to pay. Above all, I would become an enigma to my family.

I feel nothing but heartache now when I think of all the clever, angry, dissatisfied women who stalked the landscape of my youth. Weighed down with housework they seethed with resentment, which, having no outlet, snapped back into spite. You could practically see its barbs shooting out of their eyes — the 'evil eyes', whose nefarious glare my cultural forebears sought to elude by concealing their joys, lying about their successes and keeping their dreams to themselves.

These women oozed bitterness, their lives so small they took to policing one another. Each inveighed behind the other's back about who among them had gained weight; who was dependent on pills; who had suffered 'a nervous breakdown' — a phrase my mother could only utter in hush-hush tones; who had lost money thanks to her feckless husband; and whose children were cross-eyed, stupid or in need of a good hiding. Inside this ring of poison they prided themselves on their ability to find fault.

My mother was among them.

The more distance I gained on home the more she seemed to shrink into the Iraqi-Jewish recesses. Yes, she had energy and sparkle and wit, and brains to boot — which were sorely underused. But just like her peers she had no status, no public platform, no profession.

I've often wondered where my mother's considerable intellect might have taken her had she had chances in life — and I suspect that in his bones my father wondered too, since he was deeply jealous of any interests that didn't include him: if she wanted to read a book or spend the day with Marta, he'd act up. But such treats were rare. For the most part my mother's existence was consumed in juggling domestic chores and servicing my father's various needs, of which there were many.

I saw her as a dynamo back in the day, yet clearly she exhausted herself, paddling madly behind the scenes to keep the shiny surface of our lives above reproach. Knowing that if she slipped up it would be noted. First and foremost by other women.

Even more than I, my mother had been raised to serve others. When her family left Baghdad as refugees, my mother a very innocent 18 years old, she'd had to forfeit her higher education so her younger brother could take up his. When money became tight she and Marta found jobs to support their widowed mother, risking their marriage prospects being tarnished through contact with workaday realities. At Air France my mother quickly gained the confidence of her managers, earning her the sort of performance reviews that propelled male colleagues up the company ladder. But instead of being promoted she was given the task of training new female ground staff and of mollifying VIP travellers disgruntled at having their flights changed.

When she eventually did marry, at a culturally ancient 32, it was just as well. Any later and she'd have been abandoned to a life of spinsterhood. Though, on my wishful reading, perhaps she would have become a leading light in a big-name corporation and I can't help but feel that deep down she'd have preferred it that way.

Exile twists families into strange contortions. It freezes them in the moment of leaving, creates an unnatural attachment to whatever cultural baggage makes it out intact. Growing up I recognised that my Iraqi-Jewish upbringing was time-warped and antiquated. Also that any escape I made would rule out re-entry. I'd be so far removed from where I'd been formed there'd be no recognising what I'd become. But since my greater terror was that I would end up like my mother, wheels constantly spinning to little purpose, I chose the exit route, latching onto feminism as soon as it came within my grasp, desperately hoping its liberationist ideology would liberate me.

With feminism in my corner I could remake myself against type, practise a radical form of artistry, sculpt myself using bold new lines. I could shape myself into an arrow and take aim for the stars, leaving behind me all those trappings of conventional womanhood. I have feminism to thank for shooting me into higher education, out of bad relationships, into work and, eventually, a new life: and yet even as I rewired my head I recognised that something of the former programming remained.

This residue felt inescapable. I sensed it whenever I internalised a failed relationship as my own fault; when that deflating voice inside my head told me I was mad to want that job, that life, that world; when instead of complaining about being the target of male transgressions large and small I blamed myself; and when, to this day, I submerge myself in busywork because it feels safe and known. Though I know it cannot nourish me I feel the wrench of its vestigial hold.

When I think of the old program I think of 'the blind grinding of subterranean force, the long slow suck, the murk and ooze' that Camille Paglia evokes time and again to give voice to those chthonic urges to which she believes women are eternally subject. It is out of these forces, says Paglia, that life arises only to sink back again, as if returning to the swamp.

I have felt that suck and pull many times, the ineluctable tug of early conditioning encircling my limbs like vines, drawing me backwards when I've wanted to get ahead.

I discovered that I wasn't especially tribal when I set about finding a look of my own. Tribal was what I wanted to leave behind. But nor was I an out-and-out individualist: it was enough for me just to enjoy the feeling of choice and for my choices to grate on my father. I mooched around the house, sporting messy, muzzy bed hair and stinking like an ashtray, and built a collection of pantaloon-style trousers, crop tops and huge hoop earrings, alongside a clatter of palette boxes filled with glittery eye shadows. The 1980s was coming and I was going to embrace it.

My father was chagrined and he made a show of it by sniffing at my get-up whenever I left the house. But then my father's star was falling. With hot competition from innovative prêt-à-porter labels and hipster outlets such as Biba selling boho chic, he was unable to keep his West End couture business afloat.

The tail end of the 1970s found him running a whole-sale showroom in London's Whitechapel Road, selling crêpe-de-chine garments to Egyptian and Nigerian buyers who wore him out with their haggling. Though he blamed the faltering economy it was my father's lack of business acumen that finally caught up to him and no amount of clever accounting on my mother's part was sufficient to undo the many wrong-footings and miscalculations that drove him out of couture. It was a monumental slide from his heyday, when he'd sewn clothes for stars like Shani Wallis and Eartha Kitt, and aristocrats such as Lady Harewood.

Surrounded by East End rag-traders operating at the cheapest end of the business — bottom-liners who saw clothing as turnover and individual garments as *schmutter* — my father tried to sweeten the atmosphere with talk of the latest Paris fashions, frothing up his sales patter with tittle-tattle he'd read in the society pages of glossy magazines. Buffered by this harmless pomp he would issue stern reminders to his slouchy, indifferent staff about the importance of cut and lecture buyers on what a well-made seam ought to look like.

Glimmers of the old life were never quite snuffed out however and if the opportunity arose for my father to make a wonderful garment — the occasional private commission, a 'do' my mother simply had to attend — he would come to life like a marionette kitted out with new strings. His mind would be suddenly a-twirl at the prospect of dreaming up head-turning creations. Visiting his old suppliers he'd buy up sumptuous fabrics by the yard, matching them with beads and brocades, picking out linings and trimmings and threads that blended in or stood out. Undaunted by the long nights of sewing required his eyes twinkled and all the old energy swam back into his unpractised hands.

In this way I acquired the only couture dress I have ever owned, made of blood-red silk — the colour an heirloom perhaps ought to be. Its boned and thickly brocaded bustier held me reassuringly, like a dance partner. My father even constructed a box bag out of the leftover brocade.

I cannot deny how I cherished this dress. Like any well-crafted item, a Rolls-Royce engine or Fabergé egg, it was a beautifully engineered thing, in its own way a small marvel. The fact that it was mine astounded me. And yet I abhorred everything it stood for, as well as what I became when I wore it: the wished-for daughter I had decided not to be. Each time I pulled on my blood-red dress I'd be embroiled in the tussle over who or what determined me and so I wore it on as many occasions as I could as if that might settle matters — and without being sure I could get away with such flagrant self-display without becoming a parody of myself: the couturier's daughter who could boast only a single frock.

I still don't know if I wore that dress to please my father or myself. But it's clear that when my father made it for the younger me he had his own agenda.

I can't say exactly when I clocked that my parents had begun scouting for suitable husbands. But there was something fishy about the way they suddenly began taking me along to big family weddings, my father eager to introduce me around like some debutante. I would wear my red dress and he would twirl me across the dance floor, showing it off. Or showing me off.

I remember teaching him a dance that involved a hip-on-hip sashaying movement, and him gamely trying to keep up. Looking back I think the dance was a bit risqué and far from suitable for a father-daughter duo to perform. Thinking of it makes me cringe. But then so do a lot of memories from the time I was a show pony. I am more comfortable recalling how all the unspoken matchmakery on the part of my parents was already too late. I had gone my own way in my head if not yet bodily — though I occupied myself doing just that on the sly, aiming my sights at a good university that would, and did, get me out.

These days G and I joke about what might have been.

One of the potential suitors my parents encouraged me to meet, and I seem to remember that I agreed to a dinner date just for the hell of it, went on to become very wealthy. A few years ago he provided generous funding to build a new synagogue not far from the area I grew up in. It's a modern-looking, brutalist cube with rough concrete edges, and so out of place among the slouchy soot-covered terraces on either side that it may as well have landed from space. G says the synagogue reminds him of the Borg ship — the Borg being a recurring alien adversary of Captain Picard's in the *Star Trek: The Next Generation* television series. What makes the Borg so threatening is its matriarchal hive structure, assimilationist homogeneity and cyborg interdependence (everyone in the collective is a machine-like drone). The Borg is completely at loggerheads with Starfleet's rugged American individualism. Every time it succeeds in capturing an earthly enemy it absorbs them into the collective, eroding any precious autonomy.

G and I cackle conspiratorially whenever we pass the synagogue cube, having dubbed the building 'The Berg' in honour of its sci-fi homologue. But the unfunny truth beneath the gag is just how drone-like and homogeneous was the clannish culture I'd left behind. *Just think*, I tell G, mindful of the building's benefactor, *I could have been the Berg Queen.*

At some point my mother decided to put her considerable energy behind me, urging on my education, employment and eventual independence. Not being one to upset the status quo she never signed up to feminism herself, remaining out of step with the many women of her generation who did, but she saw the good it did me. How I

MARINA BENJAMIN

clung to it as to a rope swaying over the abyss.

Feminism gave my escape enough velocity to burst through my family's cultural bubble, but only just. I went to university, got myself a couple of degrees, but then sputtered and stalled, not knowing how to land myself upright in a wider world whose bearings remained largely unintelligible to me. It turned out that I had no more idea of how the working world functioned than my mother did and, though I hate to admit it, no better luck shucking off my ingrained schooling in pleasing others. I began to intuit that every step forward would involve me battling those chthonic impulses.

Perhaps this is the lot of modern women, to be forever caught between the old program and the new, striving to haul ourselves out of the mud-world of pre-feminism, continually hoisting ourselves up only to be knocked back. We're trying it on, fronting it up, projecting wildly ahead of ourselves in order to rewrite the old stories about what women can be and do, only for the ghosts of our mothers and grandmothers to body-snatch us.

Of course it's not entirely regressive to experience the many in the one. Haunted by the ghosts of women past we might take comfort in living with an inner pluralism. I know I do. It may even be the case that such 'hauntings' enable feminists to comprehend better than anyone that the struggle for self-acceptance is just as defining as the struggle for self-sovereignty.

The British artist Rachel Whiteread is a year older

52

than me — and likely shaped by similar cultural forces. I am drawn to the way her work, like mine, forever circles the domestic: it is all houses and household ephemera, bunkers and fortresses with Whiteread. As a wry commentary on how women's work is an absurdity in the context of abstract, masculine intellect I especially admire her *Modern Chess Set*, made in 2005. Its chequerboard grid is made up of alternating carpet and linoleum squares, while its pieces comprise dinky doll's house furniture. In place of rooks, kings, knights and bishops, those emblems of male power, Whiteread offers colourful plastic miniatures of equipment associated with housework. There are lampshades and easy chairs, fireplaces and vanity units, ironing boards, wash pails and an assortment of kitchen appliances, all rendered in the soft-curved moulding of playthings. There is humour in the clash of iconic symbols, but also pathos. These things don't mix: domestic life and labour do not sit well on a worldly stage dominated by men. On that stage they represent entrapment.

Whiteread's tongue-in-cheek chessboard seems to dramatise an impasse. As if to say you can move those pieces all over the board but you'll never checkmate patriarchy. You will forever be entangled, bittersweet, in the responsibilities of the home — launch pad, prison, refuge, balm.

It is only in reflecting on this work now that it strikes me that its title contains a joke — *Modern*. There is nothing modern-looking at all about those chess pieces, injection-moulded into domestic appliances. Their aesthetic is straight out of the 1950s. It makes me think Whiteread perhaps intended to comment on the way the newfangled technologies of that decade — fancy washing machines with rapid spin cycles; turbocharged vacuum cleaners — while meant to make short shrift of women's work, ended up tying women to more complex and demanding regimens of domestic labour. Or perhaps Whiteread's drift is more a remark on how little has changed, the modern woman bound as ever she was to the manacle grip of home.

Modern Chess Set forces me to admit that while I've never stopped identifying as a feminist I am less and less certain of what it means to *live* as one. I don't mean how to organise and mobilise collectively: I mean simply how to be.

When women writers I revere say that everything they write is feminist I find myself wanting details and qualifications, misgivings, regrets. I want to know what is at stake when any woman — writer, artist, lawyer, plumber or policewoman — calls herself a feminist. How explicit are her commitments? How self-conscious? What will she hazard to achieve her goals?

In middle life, increasingly I find myself lamenting what gets left out of the burnished picture that any public-facing feminist presents as she leans in and strides through the world: the hidden mechanisms necessary to maintain her persona, the concessions and trade-offs brokered on the home front. I want to know what latent energies propel, push back against, or act as counterpoints to her stated feminism.

Behind the scenes of public life does she take on the double shift or pay another woman to do it for her? Slave over family meals after she clocks off work, care for an ageing parent, prioritise the emotional needs of her circle of intimates? Does she concern herself with the injustices other women might face? Just as important, how does she carve out space in which to be herself, overriding her programming?

In the way she does these things, or doesn't do them, I want to know if she is being true to herself.

I could set the tone here. Be declarative. Tell you that as a heterosexual, cis woman who mostly passes for white I profit from a suite of unquestioned norms — though when I position myself outside the chalk circle I'm able to better see how white advantage desensitises us to other oppressions. I have things I never thought I'd have, including a husband and now-adult child (both acquired fairly late). I enjoy the kind of financial independence my mother longed for but didn't attain until it was too late to profit her. I own most of my house (with the bank owning the rest) and undertake the largest part of the physical and emotional work involved in its daily upkeep.

But this is not enough. Because every day I struggle with how to be a woman. Frequently when I speak I am not heard. Frequently I am filled with rage. Sometimes that rage is directed at women who refuse to get behind feminist causes, for fear of losing male patronage or out of a misguided belief that key battles have already been won. But mostly I am filled with rage at men — their gaze, paternalism and entitlement; the way they take up space! — never mind that I love many of them as individuals.

I rage at myself as well. For my own feminist failures. For constantly undermining myself and too-easily disappearing into the menial everyday labours women unthinkingly take on to support those around them, and hide from ourselves. For making all my moves as though I lived on Rachel Whiteread's chessboard.

1

Is the personal still political? It was the mantra of my day. To me it meant that feminism should dictate how I lived behind closed doors. It could get into my head, my bed and my body, my relationships with others and my relationship with myself. As it changed my life from within it altered the way I moved through the world. This feminism was aspirational.

But as the writer and critic Jacqueline Rose has made clear, politicising the personal is problematic. It entails driving underground everything in ourselves that fails to square up to feminist scrutiny and leads us to 'sanitise' female experience. Politicising the personal hides the darkness of women's inner lives.

In *Women in Dark Times* (2014) Rose calls for a feminism that is true to its contradictions. A 'scandalous feminism' that hugs to itself 'the most painfully outrageous aspects of the human heart'. Rose wants to make room for women's 'anguished voices' and dark inner lives, for the places and spaces to which we retreat in order 'to make sense of what impedes us' before finding the wherewithal to 'defy [our] own predicament'.

I am all for a scandalous feminism. Wayward in its nature and its talk. A feminism that throws off reason and embraces uncertainty. Such a feminism accepts self-dissolution — the way we are perpetually undone by features of our own internalised oppression. This is not collusion, which is largely unconscious; rather Rose's feminism of contradictions admits of a fragile way of being that is eternally conscious of the limits of its own power.

It makes room for Rosa Luxemburg, who
in 1898 wrote of her own fragility in a
letter to her lover Leo Jogiches, saying,
'it was precisely those bruises on my soul
that at the next moment gave me the
courage for a new life'. And it embraces
the French writer Colette, who among her
life's treasures counted the 'blows and scars'
that had taught her resilience and become a
cherished part of herself.

2

In my experience whatever dark side we
have buried has a way of reappearing.
Experiences and feelings we conceal are like
fossils deep in the ground, quietly preserved
until our lives are subject to upheaval or
internal tumult and then they are thrown up
in jagged strata, out of time and out of place.
As the topography of our inner lives shifts
with age and experience, breaking up and
buckling, the things that we most dislike
about ourselves, that we have suppressed,
or that undermine us and compromise our
ideals are suddenly exposed to the light.

Often there is growth in this re-emergence. Ask any psychoanalyst worth their salt.

In her book *Surfacing* (2019) the poet and nature writer Kathleen Jamie reworks this idea in the context of archaeology. She is concerned with what we inherit and what we lose and with how generations separated by vast swathes of time can commune with one another still — the land spilling the past into the present, the spirit world calling to us through echoes of the past retained by specific places. Jamie travels from dig to dig, from coastal Quinhagak on Alaska's western edge to the isle of Westray in the Orkneys, but the terrain she explores might just as well describe the human mind.

Jamie understands that the regurgitated past stands in for the missing parts of ourselves that make us whole. In Quinhagak it represents the hunter-gatherer existence, or old ways of living, lost in a modernity that brought new ills — poverty, depression, alcohol abuse, bad diets. Westray's Neolithic settlements, meanwhile, reveal how older buildings had been repurposed, nothing thrown away.

Time's skin is so thin in places that old and new, past and present, blend and blur.

Archaeology offers a wonderful metaphor for the layered structure of the psyche and our need to access its unexposed depths where resides the dark side of ourselves into which we shunt everything we're reluctant to face, but from which we have so much to learn. It tells me that the things we bury and that refuse to stay buried can have healing power. Can offer a truer if, at times, less recognisable version of who we are.

Compliance is a feature of masculinity too. It's just not that widely acknowledged.

Only a handful of men get to run corporations or lead nations or communities, beating out male-on-male competition for women, income or resources. Only a handful get to be heroes on the battlefield or its sporting equivalents. This much is clear. But perhaps it is more interesting to look at men who are not well served by patriarchy, among whom my father was a prime example. To the extent that I've always thought that my mother's secret desire was to be a powerbroker, a lawyer, say, or corporate strategist, then my father's unspoken, perhaps unspeakable, desire was to be a homemaker.

From earliest childhood he'd dreamt of becoming a famous couturier and dressing beautiful women, of being a purveyor of luxury and refinement, a setter rather than follower of trends. In my mind's eye I picture him at 12, sitting under the shade of a palm tree in his native Rangoon, sipping lemonade and bemoaning his rigid and parochial upbringing as the scion of an upright family of expatriate Iraqi Jews. He must have understood early on that he did not much resemble his own father, Aslan, a proper lion of a man, who could be ruthless, competitive and sometimes violent.

My father longed to escape to Europe, where he could float among artists and courtesans, stroll along tree-lined boulevards and dip into café society to sample social freedoms undreamed of in the East. He'd stake his all at the roulette wheel, try absinthe! Like a young Gatsby he must have imagined moulding himself into a creature of sophisticated tastes and pleasures.

His first move however was backwards. After the British retrenched their presence in Burma in the mid-1930s his family, fearing instability, wasted no time in flee-ing, scattering people and belongings across continents, which is how he found himself unexpectedly coming of age in glamour-parched Palestine. His late teenage years were spent desperately chasing his dream into a handful of mean corners where it had to fight for the merest breath of survival. There were trips to the dressmaker with his mother, the chance to sew evening gowns for his older sisters, the passive consumption of as much Hollywood glamour as the Eden Cinema in Jerusalem was able to screen.

Were it not for growing hostilities between Arabs and Jews, which suggested that war would not be long in coming, my father might have languished forever in his colonial backwater, straining to keep his nose up in the clouds, where he sensed the air was finer. As it was, the impending conflict over Palestine saw him bundled off to study in newly liberated Paris, carrying soft linen suits and leather luggage, while his rough and tumble contemporaries shaped up to fight for a national homeland. It was tacitly understood in my family that my father was not built to endure physical stress, much less active combat; that a certain delicacy was called for in order for him to legitimately navigate the territory of conventional masculinity.

And so fate slipped quietly into his life through the back door, freeing him to study couture and to live flamboyantly, rising late and breakfasting grandly like the artists and flâneurs he so admired.

It also freed him to be a code switcher. In the company of women, which was my father's preference, whether family friends, clients, models or seamstresses, he didn't have to perform masculinity nor was his sexuality ever in question. He could without inviting judgement be as gossipy, theatrically self-aggrandising or fey as he pleased. At his London couture house, which was arrayed across the upper two floors of a small townhouse in Quebec Street, one housing the Queen Anne–style salon, with the workroom below whirring with sewing machines and chatter, he was an impresario among his girls.

Within the privacy of our house the traditionally gendered workload fell out in novel patterns. My mother was proud but not especially houseproud and cooked only because my father couldn't, all of which created space for him to take the domestic lead. He was the one who chose not only our clothing but the household furniture, bedding, carpets and drapes. He obsessed over colour schemes, lighting and mood and presided over the social schedule, drawing up plans as to who should be invited over to show off to once everything was the way he wanted it. At weekends my mother drove him around town to visit upholsterers' studios and fabric retailers, high-end department stores and lighting and lamp specialists, while I stewed in the back seat of the Cortina.

Among the Iraqi-Jewish men who populated my parents' inner circle my father was less sure where he stood. These men used to separate out of the extended family of an evening, their stomachs full on a rich dinner, and withdraw to the living room to light fat cigars, sip whiskey and tell saucy jokes, my father joining them only reluctantly. With a child's perception, unencumbered by knowledge or doubt, I could tell he was anxious in the company of men. He didn't get their jokes or if he did he didn't find them funny. He didn't drink. And he couldn't hold his end up when the talk turned to politics, financial markets or sport. None of that world concerned him. I also picked up on the way other men eyed each other around my father, as if he were part of the joke. But since I had nowhere to put these observations I filed them away as puzzles awaiting solution.

One solution I was familiar with, even if I didn't fully comprehend my father's need for the outlet it gave him, was his explosive temper. He could be a volcano emitting noxious fumes. A pressure cooker whose valve had been loosened. A cartoon villain spitting heat. Overwhelmed by having to dance to patriarchy's tune he couldn't contain himself and when he blew he'd lash out at whatever was in his path.

In the Whitechapel years, after he discovered his business partner had been raiding the company's assets, he twisted himself into angst-ridden knots. He couldn't sleep, couldn't eat, couldn't talk about anything else. Too cowardly to confront his partner my father imploded, collapsing to the floor with a coronary. Ever the stalwart my mother was there to pick up the pieces and she stepped in to run his business during his long convalescence in hospital. I was so caught up then in my own escape and so contemptuous of what I saw as my father's weakness that I had little sympathy for his plight. Now I recognise that he and I had far more in common than I knew. Patriarchy, it seems, could fell us both.

Like my father it is sometimes enough for me just to walk through the everyday hetero-patriarchal reality of the world to be unravelled by it. I want to collapse onto the nearest public bench and weep for the lot of women

— occasionally for the lot of men. Sometimes the work of masking that feeling of fraudulence, of being an imposter in a male-dominated world, is enough. Or the sting of my own vulnerable nature is sufficient cause. Or being on the floor with exhaustion and not having the wherewithal to lift myself up.

We are used to grandiose kinds of unravelling: post-partum depression, grief and bereavement, the non-negotiable endings of significant relationships. In my own day-to-day existence I am habitually undone by my inability to sleep, when my body is subject to sweats and chills, the bedclothes rumpled with anxiety and my nerve-endings raw — alive with animal zeal. And insomnia is nothing if not grandiose. All those strung-out nights when I'm forced to stare down my irrational terrors and unmet yearnings and, much as my father confronted in himself, my insufficiencies and limitations. I have learned to ride out the experience of coming undone in sleeplessness and to work productively at the point of resistance within, for only at that point do you discover what resources you possess and, just as important, which ones you lack.

But what if the unravelling isn't so obvious? Because in my experience self-erasure sits right alongside pro-ductivity. Selfish resentments get precipitated at the far reaches of the heart, where generosity dries up. Our animal selves are perpetually primed to break through the constraints we place on ourselves and upend our carefully laid plans. It is as if the leftover bits of the old program that got spliced in with the rewrite are continually dragging us back to the swamp, even as we attempt to lift ourselves out. Out of apologising and justifying and demurring and compensating. Out of swallowing things and not complaining; out of concealing hurts and being brave in the face of failure; out of not shouting and not making a scene. Not least, out of carrying everything. Sometimes I think that carrying — other people, the continuity of history, generational identity, the emotional load of the everyday — is the main thing that women do.

I am trying to pay more attention to those moments when meltdown threatens. To the unwanted intrusions of the past into the present: the way the geological underlay of early gendered conditioning, once thrown up to the surface, can surprise us, catching us off guard with its unravelling ways. Are we still recognisable to ourselves when this happens? And if not can we learn from it?

I am also struggling to understand how if you are a man navigating patriarchy or a woman attempting to square your public and private selves you have to acquire a certain deftness of movement, taking the suit off, as it were, as you enter one door and putting it on again as you exit.

Feeding

My kitchen is the opposite of Marta's, orderly and inviting, with neat wooden cupboards painted in lime white, topped with a thick grained oakwood counter that's a little beat up with use. There's a television tucked into an alcove, bookshelves running along one wall, a patterned kilim and sagging sofa. The room doubles up as a living space, but because it is half-buried in the basement it is cave-like and earthy: a little damp, a little dark, a little love-worn.

All my days begin and end in this kitchen, from bleary-eyed mornings spent bumping inarticulately into family members as we fumble for coffee, to soft-lit nights, settling the dog down with his bowls of water and kibble before heading up to bed.

The kitchen is the heart of the house, the place that pumps love through its different chambers, lifeblood of our domestic operations. It is not just where food is made, but where care lives: all of us migrate there for tea, toast and comfort.

If cleaning is my penance, cooking is my prayer. Wash, peel, chop, spice; wash, peel, chop, spice; and so on. Ritualised, repetitive and soothing, these basic kitchen chores locate me among the humbler things in this world — the carrot, the string bean — but also the endless generations of women who've daily and thanklessly performed these very same tasks. Inserting myself into that history is to enjoy a quiet anonymity, a sense of simply being, absent of striving.

All this Marta missed out on while busy shaking her fist at the household gods. And my mother likewise, being so burdened in her case by the idea of duty that such simple pleasures eluded her.

Mostly I cook to get out of my own way — to forget myself and dissolve into the ranks of faceless womanhood. But cooking is also my go-to place for finding solace and a deep absorption. Standing at the counter with my chopping boards, knives, spice jars and pots within easy reach my cares lift as I focus on life's small and finite challenges. How thinly can I slice this onion? How much umami flavour can I get into this stew?

When it comes to feeding others I sometimes feel as if I am communicating *through* the food, extending myself towards them, almost molecule by molecule, nudging the idea of sustenance onto friendship. Perhaps all compulsive feeders feel this way, each of us beating our kitchen wings, collaboratively generating a culinary version of the butterfly effect whose rippling impacts might be felt far and wide. Safe to say, a feeder knows the value of welcome, an Old English word rooted in the passions, in *willa*, meaning pleasure or desire, *cuma* meaning guest, also *cuman* for come. Welcome is the practice of receptivity, the art of making room inside yourself so that you can be filled with more. It is an invitation to openness, to allowing life to flow in without reserve.

Given that the kitchen is the room I retreat to, for the duration of the COVID-19 lockdowns I practically lived there. In that time the oven seemed to be perpetually burning, diffusing a gentle heat, and the fridge was reassuringly full. Our small family of three, me, G and our teenager, spent long hours around the big table, bolstering ourselves against the dreadful news that drip-fed daily from our screens and leaving only to walk the dog or pick up supplies.

But another kitchen soon became central to my lockdown life. Ten minutes from my front door a soup kitchen sprung up, part of a catering company that had turned into a public-facing deli slash bakery during the pandemic. Its owner, Doug, had worked out of the same East London premises for a decade, but when the pandemic broke his supply chain collapsed. Unable to source bread he opened the bakery; after seeing supermarket shelves ransacked he started the deli. Then along came the soup kitchen, an outreach initiative catering to the growing ranks of the hungry.

G and I stumbled on this lively neighbourhood hub after we began making long exploratory visits to the deserted backstreets of the City of London. Each time we ventured out in the eerie silence to walk that square mile of impregnable white stone buildings, formerly awash with sharp-suited men and with women clacking along the pavement in killer heels, we felt as though we'd tumbled through a portal into the opening scene of a zombie movie. We'd press our faces to the dusty windows of darkened pubs and ogle artisanal shops that would likely become commercial COVID casualties: frou-frou places specialising in weird structural knits or customised umbrellas. Whichever way we turned within the maze of narrow streets the hollow echo our of footsteps followed.

We spied the soup kitchen while coming back from a frigid January excursion. It was attached to Doug's bakery, from whose doorway light and warmth emanated as from a winter's hearth. The window was crammed with stacked trays of flaky, buttery, sugary confections: turnovers and cookie wheels, mouth-watering sponges and cheesecakes, all selling for fractional sums. Then the staff behind the counter would throw in a free coffee or extra slice of cake; one time a cannister of squirty cream. What kind of business model was this?

The soup kitchen was housed inside a subsidiary kitchen space next to the bakery that was filled with giant mixers and stacked ovens, and open for service every weekday from 5.00 pm–7.00 pm. A trestle table had been set up front-of-house to hold the soup pot on its electric heater and behind it two servers in face masks were dishing up. A small gaggle of locals hung about on the pavement, queuing informally, their breath escaping in frosty puffs.

I volunteered immediately for whatever shifts Doug would give me. I had arrived at that point in lockdown when I could no longer stand my own company or the unvaried tenor of my thoughts and suddenly I knew it: wherever I turned, there I was again, my own echo and double. I could never forget myself.

In that moment outside the soup kitchen I wanted to experience not just the frisson of human connection or the rub of the unfamiliar that is the city dweller's drug of choice. I wanted to let the hurt of others in somehow. Lockdown had numbed me and I wanted to feel again.

It wasn't just the everyday intimacies afforded by touch that I missed: the glancing contact that communicates recognition, warmth, humour, understanding. But something more basic. A kind of casual interpenetration, a sloughing off of selfhood and a subtle commingling that spoke to the grittier aspects of community: the primal sting that comes with acknowledging our bodily vulnerability to contagion.

I wondered if my longing for porousness anticipated the pandemic's legacy. Could the melting together and re-melding we fear so much in disease commute into something we might enjoy in health? Might the embrace of permeability offer a more fluid understanding of how we converge and diverge, one that absorbs both our differences and commonalities? And could such a way of being offer an antidote to the 'buffered self' — that defended state which the Canadian philosopher Charles Taylor has identified as the default condition of modernity?

In a wide-ranging study published as *A Secular Age* (2007) Taylor charted the progressive disenchantment of industrialised societies as they emerged from the bog of magic and superstition into an upright world whose boundaries were rationally delimited — the various languages of science and secularism becoming over time great flood barriers in this process. He says that while reason might have bolstered us against the chaotic forces of the old spirit-infused world which threatened to overwhelm us, at the very same time it desensitised us to entire realms of experience. In becoming 'buffered' we disengaged from a vital force field and grew alienated from whatever we couldn't control.

Taylor's 'buffered self' is as good a description as any of our atomised society, through which humans move discretely and autonomously, the contents of our heads more alive to us than material reality, our individual integrity sovereign, the boundary between inside and out yet another buffer working 'to make disengagement possible'.

In such a society it is only too easy to draw a cordon

around a small circle of obligation and not extend yourself beyond it, to convince yourself that paying your taxes is the sum total of what you owe society, to unthinkingly equate community with the idea of a self-selecting group of friends. The soup kitchen was my way of forcing myself through the cordon at a time when we were being instructed to do the very opposite.

That entire countries were walling up seemed to belie our planetary interdependence even as the turn inward made sense epidemiologically. But I did not want to be buffered. I wanted to believe we were 'all in it together', one sloppy sea of humanity, rising and ebbing as one, not least because of the moral premium this placed on the individual to be accountable to the group. Ironically it was those groups of people unable to wall up, for economic or professional reasons, who best demonstrated this principle. On the front line of contagion they cared for others or worked jobs that continually exposed them to others.

Like them I wished to be mobilised: to move beyond my cordon. G had sewed face masks and delivered medications to the vulnerable, then later volunteered as a steward at a vaccination centre. But standing there on the street on that frigid January evening when we first encountered Doug's enterprise I could think of nothing I wanted more than to return to the kitchen — that most unbuffered of zones — where food, love's very own ambassador, travels in and out, awakening appetites and desires and the longing to reconnect.

Sunny is one of the regulars. An older woman with a scraggle-haired dog on a lead frayed to breaking point, she usually shows up at the beginning of a shift in search of a bit of banter. She'll say: I'm too tired today so I'll just take the one soup, otherwise I have to walk up and down and knock on door after door, and they don't answer. Why not? I ask. Most of them can't walk, she says. If they could they'd come here themselves.

Normally Sunny fills one bag with soup containers and another with bread and distributes food to as many neighbours as she can cater to across her end of the estate. Not everyone welcomes the dog. Not everyone thanks her. But she enjoys the social outing regardless: you never know who you might run into on the street. Plus it pays to stay on top of local gossip. Turns out she used to work at a soup kitchen that set up shop a borough over and she knows most of the volunteers here too. In this unofficial tour of duty the more soup kitchens you've worked the more kudos you acquire. Sunny is beloved by everyone.

In time I will come to know and admire Sunny's sense of economy, the human scale of it. If a field map were to be laid out across her days it would detail a graphic unfolding of a train of chores to be done, duties to discharge, people to tend to. I imagine its neat contours, its bullseye targets and directional arrows, a mille-feuille of IOU notes stuck on a centrally placed pin representing the countless small debts she means to honour, giving back to her neighbours, in sum if not in kind, what they have given her: spare clothes, the offer of dog-sitting, company.

Joe tends to show up most evenings too, dressed like a particular variety of wide boy that my teenager calls a 'roadman' — everything shell with added bling. His teeth need attention, but then so do mine: after almost a year of lockdown they feel furry. When I look at Joe's discoloured teeth I'm self-conscious about smiling. Joe works as a delivery rider and in between jobs he hangs out at the soup kitchen, showing up on his bike with a turquoise Deliveroo box-bag slung across his back. Sometimes he ferries leftover soup from one kitchen to another, sometimes he volunteers to serve, sometimes he's there just to chat.

Meanwhile the patrons queue politely, tactfully observing social distancing, inching forwards without jostling others. Arriving at the serving point they ask how I'm doing and I ask the same of them. We talk weather, news, the latest local sensation: sadly the neighbourhood buzz often concerns which businesses might be drawing down their shutters for good. In this and countless other small ways we skirt around an asymmetrical transaction occasioned by need — mine for connection, theirs for sustenance.

People want to know what's in the soup and how it's made, and if it's not to their liking, whether another variety is heating up out of sight on the back burner. Maybe there are even some end-of-day pastries to be had? I give them the culinary lowdown. Today we've got spicy chickpea soup with a twist of lemon, or it's roasted tomato with barley and some ingredient I can't quite identify. Today we have wild mushroom. Appealing to the palate not the purse is a nod to the moneyless nature of the transaction, for in this exchange the currency is care and the recipients patrons, not consumers.

The chatty exchanges are a reciprocal undertaking, a shared effort to shrink the gap between having and not having.

We maintain eye contact with each other: I see you, it says. I hear you. A bolt of shared recognition flies between us, a brief current of connection that zings lightly through the air, an arrow of intent. It's nice to meet you, to hear your voice, to know you're here and alive. And by the way would you like to try the soup?

———

Although the soup kitchen does not discriminate on the basis of need — anyone who fancies a cup of soup and a slice of bread is welcome to it — I soon spot which patrons are the most hard-up for cash. They are the ones missing teeth or whose hair is scraped back and dirty, their worries etched into their faces. The ones whose shoes are falling apart.

Recently a woman in her sixties, discovering the soup kitchen for the first time, stopped to ask: 'What kind of project is this?' Doug happened to be there and promptly launched into his mission statement. 'We give away food. Simple as that', he said. All he wanted was to play a part in mitigating local poverty: 'When I was making money as a chef I was unhappy', he said. 'Now I'm giving food away I feel so much better'.

After Doug left, the woman came closer, asked about the soup. Everything about her was unvarnished: she wore no make-up, her clothing was plain and worn, her talk unguarded. When I told her the soup was free and offered her a fresh sandwich she began to cry. She had had a hard time with the pandemic, she said. Her relationship had broken up and she didn't know how to make ends meet. For years she'd worked as an artist and supply teacher and somehow it had worked, but there was little call for either her paintings or her labour right now. 'I'm so embarrassed', she said, gingerly reaching for the bag of food I'd been preparing as we talked. Not for the first time at the kitchen I found myself cursing pity's contamination of charity, and the uninvited guest — shame — that it brought to the table.

In the heat of our exchange I didn't think to look at her shoes.

Natalia Ginzburg once wrote a short essay about worn-out shoes, recalling the time she'd lived alone in Nazi-occupied Rome and her shoes had fallen apart to such an extent that she could feel the icy cold of the cobbles on the soles of her feet. Whenever it rained they squelched.

And yet after the war, when she could have worn beautiful new shoes, she still went about in a risible pair. These postwar shoes of hers — worn as they were — are not as hopeless as the ones she had gone about in in occupied Rome, but they are shabby enough, she writes, to draw 'cries of indignation and sorrow' from her family. Stealing herself against their criticism she is resolute, for she has learned that it is possible to live with worn-out shoes. She has turned shame into a badge of survival.

Ginzburg cannot help wondering which way her children will go:

So, my children live with my mother and so far they do not have worn-out shoes. But what kind of men will they be? I mean, what kind of shoes will they have when they are men? What road will they choose to walk down? Will they decide to give up everything that is pleasant but not necessary, or will they affirm that everything is necessary and that men have the right to wear sound, solid shoes on their feet?

If her sons choose solid shoes then they will acquire 'the firm step of someone who doesn't give up' and if they are content with worn-out shoes they will develop 'the slow, dragging step of someone who understands what is not necessary'. Whichever way they go, says Ginzburg, it will be a choice, since shoes that do the basic, essential job of protecting one's feet do not carry a prohibitive cost. Worn-out ones can be replaced even if one is short of cash. It's more that she senses the state of one's shoes signals one's state of mind.

Take her friend who also has worn-out shoes. She is inclined to give up on it all, to stay in bed and let everything drift, 'to shut herself in some filthy bar and drink all her savings'. The shoes and the attitude are one. Ginzburg admits that she too is tempted 'to let my life go to pieces', but since she has children to take in hand she must tilt her skin-scrubbed desire to feel everything in a different direction. Still she knows that only if she remains in touch with her own vulnerable nature can she access her empathy towards others, meeting them upon that raw, rubbed-down grain of mere existence.

Ginzburg made we wish I'd paid more attention to that art teacher's shoes so I could better guess at the state of her soul and that way learn whether or not she still believed in the world's intrinsic safety.

I re-read Ginzburg's essay soon after I began volunteering at the soup kitchen and discovered that I had misremembered its gist. In my mind I'd filed away the idea that Ginzburg's worn-out shoes were emblematic of everything she had gone through, all the suffering, the uncertainty and exile, the death of her husband, the separation from her children. The shoes stood for what she had endured. On re-reading I discovered different: those battered and spent shoes were emblematic of everything she'd overcome. Triumph over hardship doesn't erase the suffering, of course, but it alters how you hold yourself going forwards.

My mother claims that you can divide people into givers and takers. Takers are depleters, people who suck you dry and choke you, who eat up all the oxygen in the room. Takers do not know when to stop. They only recognise their own privations. They live in the moment, unable to plan because all their energies go into fulfilling their immediate wants.

I learned early to be wary of takers because they were boundary raiders. In my most defended states, convinced that hiding any sign of vulnerability was key to surviving in a hard-boiled and greedy world, I recoiled from people who made their neediness known, who squeaked it into audible form, who whined, pined and bleated their sorrows: people who had no compunction about leaning hard on others, who fell apart in public. I held myself back. Privately I scoffed at their weakness. They looked almost indecent to me, these people spilling themselves.

Yet how I envied them the easy trust they placed in others and their simple faith in human nature. Beneath my aloofness I longed to be just as uninhibited, to drop into a freefall without knowing where I'd land, or throw my arms open and embrace whoever happened to be there. I wanted to know what it felt like to trust others enough to let them glimpse the soft underbelly of my vulnerability.

Givers are a rarer breed. They always seemed a mystery to me, cycling through life as a salamander might, regenerating organs, limbs and new skin and yet somehow remaining complete no matter how much of themselves they give away. Givers operate by means of an inverse law of push and pull, which argues that the more you give the more you grow. My mother is a giver (the self-sacrificing kind, occasionally given to martyrdom). G is a giver too (of the salamander cast), but I see myself as an apprentice in the giving department. My ability to nurture others, to offer them what they need without losing myself in the process, is an ongoing project.

I had worked in a soup kitchen before, when I was living a lonely, largely single life in London in my mid-twenties. Adrift and depressed I'd felt a kinship with people on society's margins. That soup kitchen was housed in a mobile van that used to pull up every Sunday evening in a vacant lot at the end of my street, its tyres crunching on the gravelly tarmac.

The kitchen catered to the local homeless population, cast out of social housing and psychiatric hospitals during the Thatcher years. When I worked there, handing out soup along with a hunk of stale bread, I befriended a soft-spoken Irish man with intelligent eyes and the pudgy features of a long-time alcoholic. After my shift the two of us used to sit on the car-park wall together, chatting about life's knocks and unexpected turns. I felt foolish and out of my depth in these conversations, short on life experience compared to his long history of living on the edge. If he showed up covered in cuts and bruises I ignored them. If he didn't feel like talking I let him be. My role was simply to be there for him.

It is hard to be meaningfully attentive to another person's needs, to dismantle the protective barriers between you. But he showed me that it can be just as difficult to sit at care's receiving end. To accept love and tenderness, esteem and gratitude — the kind of gifts that a person's faulty sense of selfhood longs to intercept and return to sender, untouched. My Irish friend was a long-time veteran of self-sabotage. Everything offered him got mangled. There were so many danger years in his frequently derailed life, when he could see he was out of control, drawn to destructive behaviours, unable to exert choice, that he lived on the inside of an emotional contradiction. He was both in peak need of care and at peak inability to accept it.

Beneath his need was a simmering resentment at

life's general unfairness — at his lot, at my privilege. One night he followed me home from the bus stop and suddenly lunged for my bag before running off into the dark, never to be seen again. I felt stunned, like I'd been tasered, though I knew I would not be calling the police. I've always understood the mugging as a punishment. Felt deep down that he didn't really want my money so much as he wanted a trust and assurance I was unwilling to give and that he didn't know how to elicit. I sensed I'd failed him.

Equality has to be one of care's ambitions. Which is to say the outcome of caring is as important as the impulse. In a caring society people in need should not have to go without basic provision, without food, shelter or warmth, while people who have more than is necessary to their comfort should donate their surplus: money, furniture, food, clothing.

But equality comes in assorted flavours. There is material equality, based on the sharing of resources, and legal equality, which insists on the same rights for all. Then there's relational equality. This denotes the kind of eye-to-eye equivalence that's grounded in the fundamental respect that one human holds for another. It doesn't matter if you are rich or poor, employed or unemployed, Right-leaning or Left; if two people can find a place to stand that allows them to regard one another with dignity

— even if it's on either side of a soup pot — then in relational terms they are equals. This is what I went looking for and to some extent found in Doug's kitchen.

Some of our most trenchant inequalities are of the relational kind, the result of those of us who can afford to do so hiving ourselves off from everything we don't want to see. We inhabit silos. Do our utmost to avoid confronting another person's pain. In an emotive essay that calls out the myths we weave around people in need Richard V. Reeves, a senior fellow at the Brookings Institution in Washington DC, argues that relational equality is the foundation of a fair and just society because if someone believes that they are better than someone else they will never see that person as fully human. Nor will they admit that, at root, material inequality has structural causes.

As Reeves puts it: 'Those who are economically productive and successful often do not see a broken labour market, which, after all, continues to work for them. They see broken people, making bad choices, who are less worthy of respect.' They see fecklessness, irresponsibility and idleness, when in reality people are ground down and excluded. They see a lack of gumption in the face of prevalent opportunity. Snowflakes instead of troupers.

At the soup kitchen one guy I volunteered with told me about two nearby churches that together with the soup kitchen made up a local triangle of food providers. What transpired was not that people visited each in turn, with the aim of hoarding supplies, but that they came with bikes or cars, alone and in groups, to cart food from one place to the other, setting up a kind of impromptu redistribution service. Their concern was with levelling. Such actions are not just about redistributing wealth (in this case food) but about paying care forwards. This is what Sunny was up to in taking more soup than she needed in order to pass it on to others in greater need than she — people whose lack of mobility prevented them from answering their doors. This is how the food chain should work.

Those would-be critics in Richard V. Reeves's sights — the ones who see broken people instead of broken markets — are the first to caution against giving downtrodden groups what they need, for fear of creating dependency. I do not buy this line of thinking any more than I buy the argument that people are fundamentally selfish or that there is no society, only competing individuals. A world that sidelines our instincts for cooperation, reciprocity and altruism: that, to me, is the real zombie-movie scenario.

In any case the Right-leaning conservatives who, generally speaking, are the ones to pipe up to denounce so-called 'benefit spongers' have got the argument back to front. It is not by caring that you create unhealthy dependencies but by not caring, and by disrespecting those who have less than you do. In a classic example of piling precisely this kind of insult on top of existing injury consider the food packages the UK government grudgingly issued to children entitled to free school meals in 2020 when schools were shut down because of the pandemic. Disrespect was stamped all over those packages. You could practically smell it rising off the spongy bread and sweaty processed cheese.

The missing element in such botched attempts to manage differential needs is compassion — the word deriving from Latin, from *com* and *pati*, meaning to suffer with. Without compassion there can be no empathy. And without empathy no inward understanding of what the psychoanalyst Adam Phillips and historian Barbara Taylor have called 'the part of ourselves that we are most disturbed by, the part that knows how much assurance and (genuine) reassurance is required to sustain our sense of viability'. If we accept this essential vulnerability in ourselves we begin to see it in others and then it becomes much harder to shrug off fellow feeling and rejoice in separation.

As I see it the unbuffered human compassion that soup kitchens serve up belongs to the dynamics of optimism. It throws down a challenge to social atomism, to heightened individualism and the uncaring society, and kindles feelings of fellowship. Although I recognise that soup kitchens, if not themselves the product of laissez-faire capitalism, in many ways help to sustain it — as private charities set up to tackle the shortfalls created by poor state provisions. Notwithstanding, the soup kitchen is where I found hope.

I'm not saying that everyone should volunteer at a

soup kitchen at least once in their lives (though it isn't a bad idea). Or even that volunteer work should be a mandatory public service in a post-pandemic world (an even better idea). But as 'normal' life returns I want to remember what was deeply felt, what was pleasingly abnormal from that time, and to keep being nourished by it.

Disposition (noun)
  1. A person's inherent qualities of mind and character.
     e.g. 'Your sunny disposition has a way of rubbing off on those around you.'
  2. The way in which something is placed or arranged, especially in relation to other things.
     e.g. 'The plan shows the disposition of the rooms.'

(source: Google)

Unlike my mother, who is an unreconstructed essentialist, the Berkeley-based psychologist Alison Gopnik believes that the give and take that most people associate with character is not constitutional but developmental. In the book she is currently writing, *Curious Children, Wise Elders*, she argues that care is a type of intelligence. A competence we can acquire once we have passed the ego-driven stage of our lives when we're always wanting more, more, more! — which drive she attributes to the kind of 'exploitative' intelligence that shapes the ambitions of youth.

As with the staged development model of Erik Erikson, care in Gopnik's schema emerges as a virtue associated with maturity, a virtue that we can cultivate through our selfless actions in the world. It's an attribute Gopnik most frequently sees among people who've reached what she calls 'elderhood'. But of course care brings its own reward since by extending ourselves towards others we prompt a reciprocal kindness.

Gopnik's ideas appeal to me in casting selflessness as capacious rather than flattening, welcoming rather than depleting. They chime with the view that for accomplished givers the more you expend yourself the more room you create for genuine growth.

It is said that money breeds money. But perhaps it is also true that kindness breeds kindness, no matter that the one concerns accumulation and the other, disposition:

Disposition (noun)

3. The formal act of giving something away.

Confession. My fridge is full of miniature pots containing food items that I am trying to save from rot. Tiny portions of herbs, a quarter of an onion, a single tomato that is going soft. I like to challenge myself to figure out what I can cook that will use everything up. But G is always teasing me about my collection of soon-to-expire leftovers and orphaned vegetables. 'Can I throw this out now, please?' he'll ask me, holding up for my inspection some wilting leaf, or a used tea bag. Absolutely not, I tell him, without even checking what he wants to dispense with.

G thinks that I have internalised the anxiety of my parents' exile from Iraq, that I cannot throw out a near-mouldering vegetable or get rid of that slick of week-old vinaigrette for fear that come the pogrom or the revolution, or for that matter the poisoned air and rising waters of climate change, I might just conceivably need it.

In the opening pages of her book *Index Cards* Moyra Davey complains that a full fridge is just one more thing to manage. The rearranging and organising and prioritising it calls for, to say nothing of all the chewing it demands, weighs on her soul. She longs to uncover 'as much of its clean, white, empty walls as possible'.

I recognise the escapist allure of a brutalist minimalism. I do. Especially when set against the cluttered reality of our lives: all that 'padding' that, as Davey complains, we're continually digging ourselves out of only for it to pile up again just as quickly — in the fridge, as everywhere else.

But for me, and for the many women I know who like to keep their fridges well-stocked, an empty fridge is too uncomfortable a reminder of our systemic precarity, of how much harder it is for women to get and hold on to things, attain financial security, plan for their futures. A full fridge is our guard against potentially devastating collapse, perhaps even destitution.

When friends moan to me about their menfolk, too incompetent to shop for food and fill the fridge, who live on boy-scout diets of one-pot-a-week lentil bakes, or the urbane equivalent — quails' eggs and champagne: but nothing else — I would say, think again. Because gendered economic disparity is the more likely culprit. Men are simply more confident that when they need food they will get it. They don't require the security blanket of a full fridge since women will cater to their needs, feeding them and as often as not cleaning up after them too. It may be an inefficient way to live, but then most men can afford to be inefficient, cultivate inefficiency even, given how it frees up their brains for 'real' work.

I admit that G has my number. He is aware that the prospect of lack, of there being nothing to conjure with in the fridge, makes me anxious. A shortage of nourishment exposes need unduly, renders its outline visible and makes me uncomfortable. And when the need to sate hunger goes unmet it becomes a stand-in for all those other unmet and unmeetable needs — especially those we cannot articulate. Before you know it you are being tugged into a gaping chasm of bottomless need.

G thinks that at the heart of my layered relationship with food I am trying to shield myself from having to stare down naked need. This is true, though I'd counter that I am also guarding against the complacency that comes from being excessively cushioned by a world of plenty.

I simply cannot fall under the thrall of surplus — of a culture in which wealth is measured by what you can afford to discard. I've long had a tendency to romanticise self-reliance and material austerity and I am mindful of that now as I reflect on the joys of finding more in less. Like Natalia Ginzburg I believe there are 'little virtues' to be discovered in mild privations — in worn-out shoes or endurable hunger, in feeling cold so as to better appreciate the luxury of warmth, or in having to save and pinch pennies to buy something you covet.

But the virtues of these privations are only accessible if you have privilege, which is to say when they are chosen. I have a warm home to return to at the end of my soup-kitchen shift when many of its patrons do not; Ginzburg could at any time in her postwar life easily have bought herself new shoes. Nevertheless, affecting not to know that other people suffer more than you do, buffering yourself against their pain and discharging yourself from any duty to relieve it, borders on the immoral.

Walling up might feel self-protecting but it precludes true fellowship.

Caring

After my father died following years of slow decline, his baggy sac of a heart finally giving out, my mother found herself suddenly free. For a few giddy weeks she floated on a tide of incredulity, scarcely able to believe that from now on she could leave the house when she wanted, eat whatever took her fancy or snatch a quick nap after lunch. The heavy lines she'd acquired over the half-decade in her seventies when she'd served as my father's primary carer seemed to vanish overnight. She appeared light, almost radiant, the years peeling off her like silver cleaned of its tarnish. You would never know she had just turned 80.

In those uncertain days in which she felt wobbly with possibility she drove over to see me and sat in my living room, emanating an unsteady energy.

'I just don't know what to do with my time', she said,

the longed-for liberty, now at last hers, sitting upon her like an encumbrance.

'I don't know, Mum', I said, 'you could see more of your friends, go to the movies, travel? Maybe you could visit Jacob'. At 73 my mother's younger brother had emigrated with his family from Manchester to Israel. After an unsettled start he had bought and renovated a *moshav*, or small working farm, and was constantly inviting my mother to come see it.

She shot me a withering look that said *as if* and in that moment I saw things as they were, glimpsed the weight of what was to come.

My mother had pitched up in my living room because she had no friends to fall into step with, sharing lunch, playing bridge, gossiping. There were cousins she occasionally brunched with; a couple of neighbours she was reluctant to draw close. My mention of the cinema met with a sneer — beside her existential concerns it was frivolous. As for travelling alone, well, I ought to know that unlike her brother she had no appetite for late-life reinvention, that it was my father, not her, who'd been the adventurous one.

Back in the day my father had constantly urged her to travel, even when he was too unwell to undertake it. Feeding his own wanderlust he lobbied her with racy plans. 'Let's go to Africa', he'd say, his eyes dreamily dilating as he pictured fire-coloured horizons over cracked earth, and the cooling mocktails he'd sip under a hot sun.

But my mother was immoveable. And now here she was, in front of me, in her neat cashmere sweater and pearl necklace, flashing her film-star smile — an undiminished asset — because there was only one person with whom she wished to occupy the endless hours now sprung wildly free: me.

After Marta died my mother trained her hopes of companionship on me like a heat-seeking missile. It was a desperate lunge and she knew it and felt bad about it, insisting she didn't want to burden me. I knew it too and felt bad about bridling. But we both understood there was no one else.

As I recollect this fork-in-the-road moment a memory comes to mind from long ago. I am in a training pool with my mother, who'd been taking adult swimming lessons with limited results, her attempts at breast stroke repeatedly collapsing into a hopeless doggie paddle. As she swims towards me, splashing and thrashing and gulping, she panics, and then all at once she is clinging to my neck and dragging me under, her arms flapping over my head and shoulders as she gasps for air. Half-drowned, overwhelmed, I'm convinced that I lack the wherewithal to move the two of us out of one necessary element and into another.

Now I persuaded myself that my mother needed a project. Here was her chance, perhaps just a brief window of opportunity, to rediscover something of the self she had sacrificed to the job of looking after my father. Six years of her life. Six back-breaking years of servitude and surrender, during which time she'd looked to neither her own reward nor pleasure. But the only thing she seemed interested in was mastering the online shop. She wanted velvety trousers, easy joggers, silky tops and bobble hats. Towels that still fluffed up after multiple washings. She wanted trainers she could mosey round the house in and fancy shoes for 'good wear'. She wanted perfumes with names like Opium and J'adore. 'I like to smell nice, even if I'm not going anywhere', she told me.

Caught up in a vicarious excitement for my mother I failed to see that she'd succumbed to the 'carer's curse', growing so alienated from herself over years of indenture that she'd lost sight of who she was, much less what she might want. The shopping was a giveaway: beneath her button-pressing compulsion, she no longer knew what it was she truly desired.

She put me in mind of a newly released prisoner, thrust back into society after being handed the clothes and small change that had been in their possession the day they were locked up; talismanic bearers of identity, time-shrivelled into sorry reminders of things lost, never to be regained. Outside the gates of her mind's own prison my mother remained captive, suddenly and rudely out of step with a changed world she was ill-equipped to navigate.

As I urged her to downsize her living arrangements I could almost taste the release that would flow from her relocating from a four-bedroomed house that would soon be unmanageable to a one-, maybe two-bedroomed flat she could furnish according to her own lights — though it's hard to say how much projection was involved. How my own fantasy of simply packing up and moving my minimalist dream-self into a streamlined space of my own got in the way of things.

I held tight to those moments when she seemed fired by the idea. 'I never wanted a big garden, you know, that was your father', she said. And: 'of course I'd need a spare room so the grandchildren can visit'. Nestling in next to her on the sofa we scrolled through estate agents' websites. Up popped garden flats and Victorian conversions, modern apartment blocks and new builds; there was the occasional refurbished church or school, and a whole range of accommodations euphemistically termed 'independent living'.

I could see the cogs turn as her mind weighed the inducements of novelty against the ease of continuity. But then her eyes narrowed. She started to roll worry-balls in front of the potential gateway, concerning the number of steps to climb, the security of the building, the heating costs, services costs, contingency costs. At some level I already knew that I wouldn't succeed in sparking any lasting resolve. Ducking in and out of high-spec rooms online we pondered soft furnishings and entered into animated debates over colour schemes. My mother found fault with everything.

'It's too late for me to start over', she kept saying, until I believed it too.

Ten years on, my fears have been realised. My mother can no longer manage the big house on her own and has begun to lean more decidedly on me to take care of the basics: doing her accounts and paying the bills, organising cleaners and tradesmen, managing her dealings with the local council. I bring food over when I shop, fetch her cash, accompany her to the doctor, chiropodist and dentist — and to increasingly frequent hospital appointments. After she fell backwards against the living-room wall and experienced a brief blackout we had a chair lift installed.

There are now hand grips in the bathroom. A plastic shower chair in the bath perches on rubberised matting. An expensive electrical system operates her bed, effecting a slow-motion bronco buck, which helps my mother get on and off the mattress. She has a remote-controlled fan, an array of inhalers and a high-tech hearing aid all within arm's reach. Also a super-attentive GP who pings my WhatsApp about various checks he's lined up for her — a merry-go-round of X-rays, ECGs, echoes, ultrasounds and lung-capacity tests.

We are now squarely in the realm of contingency planning. There's a key safe on an outside wall, an alarm bracelet around my mother's wrist and a list of people to call in case of emergency sellotaped to the inside of a cupboard door. For now we're okay. But the shape of now has a way of suddenly shifting.

Round and round my anxious brain loops W. B. Yeats's famous line 'Things fall apart; the centre cannot hold'. The situation with my mother is fraying and precarious. The sheer effort required to maintain the appearance of sameness has, on account of her steadfast resistance to change, introduced a volatile instability into the system. The delicate ecology we've created around her to generate a feeling of homeostasis could collapse at any time.

I talk to Julia while pushing a supermarket trolley along the aisles, my neck crooked awkwardly into the phone.

Do you drive, I ask her … Oh, good, because I don't and it would be such a help if you could drive Mum to local appointments.

Can you cook? … No? That's a shame because my mother struggles in the kitchen. She's not able to stand on her feet for very long and has been living off oven-ready meals.

Are you okay with starting one day a week because my mother isn't convinced she needs a carer at all … That's right, her basic health is pretty good … It's so helpful that you've got room to be flexible.

Have you worked in a private capacity before? I see, you've already got a client … She's 93 and still living at home! … Ah, she employs you just three days a week.

What kind of help do you offer your client? … Yes, I do understand. It is too much to have to push a wheelchair to the shops each day and then carry her shopping as well. My mother is slow, but she is still physically independent. There'll be no wheelchair to reckon with.

I think it's best if you come over and meet her, then she can give you an idea of how she spends her days … That's right, she doesn't always realise when she needs help.

Do you have references?

On days when my mother doesn't need care, as such, could you help out with some light housework?

How do you know Marlena, who recommended you?

How does a 10.00 am start sound to you, because my mother takes a long time to get ready in the mornings?

Can you do Mondays?

I've no idea what Julia truly feels about my brisk inter-rogation, but if it's pique she hides it well, tucked away behind her greater need for work.

My mother claims that I forced Julia on her and I suppose I did. Nor were my intentions wholly straightforward. I didn't just want someone to take on 'menial' tasks. I wanted my mother to understand that a carer is not there solely to do icky jobs, helping out with toilet duties and bathing, dressing and undressing, being the medication commandant. I wanted her to see that a large part of care is about companionship. A good carer is a listening post, sympathiser and administrative assistant, someone to consult, canvass or simply chat to. Carers are the advance guard, feeling out potential dangers and defusing them; occasionally they're the fall guy, jumping into the path of those dangers so their wards don't have to. I told my mother that I had become such a carer and that I felt overextended. That I needed to ring-fence more of my time. She agreed to give Julia a tryout.

Julia, it turned out, was 68. 'But I have a lot of energy', she said. She was seated in my mother's living room, her folded, wiry frame barely taking up space on the sofa, and although Julia appeared not to notice I am pretty sure my mother scoffed at her words.

Julia was well educated. She'd worked in the NHS for 20 years as a technician in a biomedical lab and for another five in a care home. When I asked why she wished to continue working now she'd formally retired she said: 'My principle in life is to help people'. This is a

Christian principle, rooted in the belief that there is value in servitude, and dignity in subsuming one's will to the will of another. I should have realised there and then that she and my mother would never find common ground. My mother disdains charity. She doesn't want to be the pitiable object on which Julia can exercise her virtue: she wants the kind of respect that comes with hierarchy.

She wants to be Julia's boss.

If you are fortunate enough to live to an advanced age, at some point you will be forced to rely on other people. You will enter that dread arena of dependence where compromise lurks around every corner and dangers too — heightened risks, unwanted intimacies, vulnerability, exposure, resentment. My mother is allergic to this kind of dependence and because she has bought into the myth that asking for help is a sign of weakness, the more she feels herself losing her grip the more she projects an outward image of strength and self-reliance.

'I don't need a carer', she protested after Julia had left, having spent the morning cooking and cleaning for her, doing the shopping and attempting to make conversation. Because care is something one is required to submit to, my mother wants nothing to do with it. Especially not the version Julia practises, which flips everything my mother believes in on its head. Above all the idea that it is in submission that true strength lies.

'Paying for help' is another story. In paying for help you are not making any concession to weakness: you are just exercising your purchasing power like any consumer. The way my mother sees it Julia is someone to be inducted into her world, the place where she rules supreme. Where it is up to her how the sheets get ironed, when meals get served and whether the living room needs a deep clean. In this scenario my mother can strut (figuratively) through the days being directive. What she cannot understand is that her top-down approach shuts the door on reciprocity.

The day after Julia's tryout my mother called me. 'I don't want her', she said, 'she's too old'.

'But Mum you've said yourself that you don't need Julia to do any heavy-lifting work?'

The comment flew right past her.

'Do you know what she said to me', said my mother. I girded myself for the dismissal that was sure to come. 'She asked if she could come and live with me. Imagine that. She wants *me* to look after *her*!'

You've clearly given your mother a get-out clause.

What do you mean?

Well, with other people in your life you seem to be learning where to draw a line, but from everything you've told me about your mother you have decided not to refuse her demands.

That's true. Because I want to honour my duty of care and do it with love. The trouble is I feel importuned by her and then I'm flooded with guilt.

You can't have it both ways.

But she calls me every day, sometimes twice a day, with

the smallest of concerns.

They're not small to her.

No — but she has this way of stopping me in my tracks. She makes these announcements then leaves them hanging: 'I've got diarrhoea', she'll say, or 'my iPad's not working'. Then she expects me to jump to.

You have to train yourself to ask 'Is this an emergency?' and if it isn't to tell her that you're in the middle of work and you'll call her back. In fact, agree an assigned time.

Well, I can see how the tactic might work if she was specific about things, but most of the time she's got this ominous, stick-shaking way of intimating that things need to be done.

You need to tell her what that feels like for you.

I've tried, but practically every time I check the answering machine there'll be a new message saying: 'there are a few important things I need to tell you'. She is expert at parking her anxiety with me.

It's up to you. You have to decide where your boundaries are.

My mother and I are doomed never to see eye to eye in our approach to ageing. All our future-oriented discussions are riven with cross-purpose. Whenever the subject of her late-life care is up for review she rails against the idea that I might one day put her in a home, as if I mean to cast her off, leaving her there 'to rot' (her words). Her stake-in-the-ground protest is absolute. *Over my dead body!*

She is convinced that she will suffer neglect in the very place designed to furnish support. She thinks she will feel lonely in the midst of community and that this will hasten her end. 'I don't want to be around old people', she complains at her most irascible, wholly unaware that acting as if her life has not changed at all is what has left her so lonely until now.

My mother believes her wellbeing will be better served by freedom than by companionship. My own inclinations run counter-wise. The choices we're granted at her stage of life are stark, but forced to take a side I'd choose company. I'd take the care home — even if it meant surrendering my independence.

It's not that I don't cherish independence, but how independent can a 90-year-old really be? The brutal slap-down of having my freedom exposed as illusory at that age would be more than I could bear. I know this because I have watched my mother's wincing disbelief as that veil was rent from her own eyes. How much self-rule can you exercise when you cannot walk 20 feet without panting and wheezing? When you are not even aware of the things you can no longer see or hear or comprehend? When your short-term memory perpetually slithers from your grasp and your knees are so swollen that every step heralds pain?

This is my mother's plight. But despite her secret (therefore instantly retractable) admission that she is not the autonomous being she once was she has maintained the illusion of competence because I have let her. I have been complicit insofar as I have allowed her world to remain unchanged. Whatever lack has appeared I have rushed to fill it. I've reframed every concession as a bold new choice. Picked up the slack. Been her ears, eyes and hands and sometimes her surrogate brain. And I do all this because I love her.

It has left me ragged.

I cannot count the times I've forgone bathing in order to meet work deadlines and still attend to her needs.

How often I've had to eat junk on the fly, left my house in a tip or been forced into the impossible position of having to choose between my teenager's needs and my mother's. I am bone-tired at the end of a tour of daughterly duty.

All of this I keep from my mother. And more besides: my whole inner life is now something I contain when I'm around her. I have become a palimpsest, effacing my own story so that I can accommodate my mother's script. At first it was effortful, this withholding. It felt like a refusal to share and it generated a distance between us that's only hardened over time. Yet my mother has hardened too. She is less and less minded to enquire about my concerns, my health, my marriage, my work, as if acknowledging my other life would force her to face up to the inadmissible knowledge that I might not be endlessly emotionally available to her.

I bite my tongue. I tell myself this is not about me. That time is short for her. That I need to be gracious, patient, sensitive, giving and kind. Above all, that I need to find some way to divest our interactions of expectation, since our relationship will never again be what it once was: confiding, intimate, mutual.

More than anyone, I know that there is no virtue in the care I offer my mother. Every time I fail to conceal my annoyance at her slowness or bristle at a thrice-repeated question I am cognisant of how far I fall short of selfless-ness. It is one thing to tamp down the naggings of ego, setting your own aspirations and desires to one side on behalf of a loved one. But this temporary muffling of the self falls far short of its transcendence, a kind of liberation that Iris Murdoch seems to have been reaching for with the concept of 'unselfing'.

Murdoch touches on this idea all too briefly in *The Sovereignty of Good* (1970), taking an example drawn from nature. She talks about being in an 'anxious and resentful state of mind' and then looking out of the window and catching sight of a 'hovering kestrel'. The sheer beauty of the bird, wings outstretched, effortlessly suspended, lifts her out of herself. It fills her mind. Leaves her exalted. 'In a moment everything is altered. The brooding self with its hurt vanity has disappeared. There is nothing now but kestrel.' For a brief moment the self is so porous it is subject to external override, a torrent of joy washing away the cloudy internal weather.

I struggle to find moments of joyful unselfing in the drudgery of daily care, though now and then I manage to absent myself from the task in hand and float away from my own concerns. If I wanted to dignify the experience I might invoke the Christian concept of kenosis, a kind of self-emptying that takes place not so that one can fill up the tank again with some higher thing, but so that one becomes transparent like a window or a ghost. You are functionally present and yet somehow profoundly absent.

But I do not particularly want to dignify my labours, which are more self-obliterating than transformative: I have to flatten myself into a two-dimensional being and rub off all my corners in order to be with my mother these days. And I am no saint. More and more I resent being her backstop.

A loving friend who eventually committed her own mother to a care home has been looking out for me. 'This is only going one way', she said recently, 'and if you keep stepping in to cover for her trip-ups and failures she'll end up eating you alive'.

The slide into self-oblivion happens by imperceptible degrees. That is what makes it so dangerous. The small ministrations, the constant vigilance, the endless availability easily slip from view, becoming part of the taken-for-granted fabric of things. This care slips under the radar because its aims are modest. Because it seeks merely to keep everything the same. The philosopher Ivan Illich was right in pointing the finger at care work as a chief example of the blunt end of the industrial economy: neglected, exploitative, largely non-monetised and incrementally 'self' eroding, he called it 'shadow work'.

I have so well disguised my own labour that even my mother, its chief beneficiary, cannot see it. I have rendered it wholly invisible. In one of the many exchanges in which I've tried to urge a new Julia on her, tried to tell her that I am finding it all a bit much, she retorted, 'What do you even do?'

Where are you feeling the tension?

It's hard to describe. There's a tightness in my chest. Plus I get headaches. But mainly just thinking about my mother generates anxiety.

Stay with the feeling. Don't theorise it.

Okay … Well, I feel almost lightheaded, but not in a good way, not like happy, trippy light-headed, more out-of-control light-headed. Sometimes I feel panic rising up my throat.

Great. Hold on to that because that is information.

Yes, but how do I use it?

Whenever you feel that bodily tension it is a signal that you need to think about boundaries.

Every now and then I am arrested by a painful compassion for my mother, the tug of a phantom umbilicus transmitting her losses and frustrations, the sheer pathos of her creeping decrepitude. I sense it in my own body as a kind of burning, an acid wash of my insides, and I have to stop whatever I am doing and let the stinging pass.

I watch her walk from one room to another, a tiny white-haired figure, limping slightly on account of her bad knee, her frame keeling to the left because her spine curves that way, her hearing aid efficiently hooked over one ear lobe. I notice how slow she has become, her body and brain sludge-like, the world made murky and confusing, its vital signals intercepted by tinnitus and by the high-pitched whine of her sonic aid. I see how she winces in discomfort when she sits down in her mechanised armchair — the kind that slides a cushioned support pallet under her legs and lets her recline at the touch of a button. I picture her eating meagre meals alone in the kitchen with the radio on too loud and imagine her going to bed at night in her immaculate white cotton nightie, frilled at the armholes, setting her reading glasses down on her bedside table next to her painkillers and water glass and anti-vertigo medication, too weary to read a book. I pray that her sleep is untroubled but I know better. I know that between her bad back and her joint-swelling arthritis it is difficult to find a position of comfort. I know that sometimes she inadvertently swallows her spittle and ends up half-choking. That she is often beset by nightmares in which she is stuck somewhere or incapacitated, in which she hollers and no one comes. That she sometimes wakes in the night feeling dizzy and confused and cannot trust herself to get to the bathroom. That once awake she cannot easily return to sleep, her mind ambushed by worries she cannot voice by day.

When I imagine her night-time terrors I am gripped by a paralysing fear that she might tumble out of bed and injure herself or trip on her way to the loo or — heaven forbid — die in her sleep when I am not there. I experience this fear as a mental landslide, exposing a chasm of dread that drops away sharply into vertiginous nothing-ness. And this chasm is just ahead of where I am standing.

At moments like these I feel my mother's anguish as my own. Her flesh is my flesh. Her pains and ailments mine. The decades between us collapse like a train of dominos and suddenly we are interchangeable, molecularly transmissible, her destiny and mine forever fused. My mirror neurons are working overtime.

Mirror neurons light up the higher brain when acts of imitative, or mirroring, behaviour take place: I yawn when I see you yawn. If you are giggling I might find it impossible not to laugh as well, or I'll tear up when I see you cry. Important in prompting empathy, mirror neurons are also involved when it comes to learning through replication and repetition. As the psychologist Louis Cozolino argues in *The Neuroscience of Human Relationships* (2006) they may originally have evolved to facilitate such learning by synchronising group behaviours such as hunting or migration, coordinating individuals so that they behave as one.

The message here is that we are wired to be co-dependent, networked into a delicate lattice of connections. Everything we do to try and forget this fact is merely part of an enabling fantasy of autonomous, self-directed personhood, which the grunt work of caring exposes as just that, a fantasy.

In therapy I return over and over to my difficulties in forming and maintaining boundaries. While I've come to understand many of the factors in my personal history that have made this a challenge for me I think that there is something fundamentally unboundaried about the care relationship, because in caring you can't help but entrust something of yourself to the other person and at the same time you absorb something of them into your own being.

When the phantom cord between my mother and me is finally cut I fully expect there to be an audible accompaniment. A tortured squeal of separation.

During the various lockdowns occasioned by the pandemic my mother was uncharacteristically upbeat. She accepted the house arrest imposed by government on the elderly and infirm without protest — the previous two winters, in which she'd barely left the house anyway, having served as a trial run. With her age qualifying her for priority home-delivery slots from overstretched supermarkets she knew she wouldn't starve. Plus her cleaner gamely agreed to wear a mask and keep on cleaning.

The bonus for my mother was that G and I were suddenly more available. Our 'bubbling up' with her guaranteed weekly visits. And if in truth there was little choice but to bubble — my mother's reliance on me to be her real-world avatar by this time a necessity — we all pretended the decision was elective.

Her good cheer was genuine and born of a rare feeling

of fellowship. In lockdown she found solidarity since now everyone else was isolated too and feeling by turns trapped, bored, challenged or defiant, just as she was. Everybody was obliged to be resilient in their outlook, active in structuring their days and — if they weren't too busy marshalling toddlers, home-schooling children or else trapped in abusive relationships — creative in occupying the empty hours. My mother's loneliness was diluted through being shared and she found herself more connected to the idea of community than ever. It buoyed her.

Alarm only set in as restrictions were loosed. Tentatively children returned to school. Capital resumed its flow through the veins of the economy while people gingerly unmasked in public, smiling shyly at seeing naked faces anew. Once life resumed, my mother's housebound existence again began to chafe. Once again it felt more like imprisonment. Once again she'd been left behind.

Her response has been to double down on her retreat from the world and turn shielding into a philosophy to live by. Come hell or high water she will not be winkled out of her home. I cannot persuade her to go for the shortest walk or to sit in the garden on a sunny day. Her engagement with the outside world is now at a minimum and always mediated — by the telephone, the iPad, and by me.

When I visit her I have grown accustomed to stilling myself so that no outside gust of vitality can come in with me, jarring the atmosphere within. Upon entering her house I strip myself down and enter an airlock, decontaminating myself from my life's interest before stepping into her sterilised zone. My lack of intimacy with her is a more effective mask than any piece of surgical gauze.

Recently I came across an insight of Arlie Hochschild's, the sharpness of which cut though me like a knife, so accurately did it describe the way my mother has shrink-wrapped her world. Hochschild, a University of California Berkeley sociologist, burst into public consciousness after publishing *The Managed Heart* back in 1983, when she coined the term 'emotional labour' to describe workers ostensibly remitted for one thing but whose actual job rests on unpaid psychological work. Retail workers instructed to smile when greeting customers are a good example, or flight attendants required to be gracious to obnoxious passengers and to put up with their endless microaggressions. Three decades later Hochschild wrote a follow-up book *The Outsourced Self* (2012) in which she revisited the emotional dynamics underpinning paid work, but this time her focus was the marketisation of love and care, of paying strangers to undertake intimate work. What does it feel like, she wonders, to leave your own cares at the door of an elderly or disabled person or infant and give yourself up to caring for them?

Among the care workers who open up to Hochschild Rose's story is especially affecting. A 'household manager' for the wife of a real-estate millionaire, Rose is babysitter and PA. She oversees a household staff comprising cooks, maids, nannies, gardeners and chauffeurs and manages all the family's travel arrangements, lavish entertainment schemes and endless home improvements. Rose is so good at her job that most of the time Norma, her employer, barely notices her presence. As Hochschild remarks: 'Rose didn't simply accomplish the tasks assigned to her; she created a smooth, calm emotional landscape through which her clients could glide unfazed.' The performance of such emotional labour is hard to see. But it takes its toll on Rose, who ends up absorbing the anxiety that would consume Norma herself if she were on the front line of her own life and not being shielded by Rose.

However, the insight that really shook me concerned the effects of this emotional outsourcing on Norma herself. Since Rose was regularly in situations in which the very essence of her job was to 'transfer sympathy' to other household employees who felt undervalued or distressed, and to do this on Norma's behalf, Norma had 'effectively purchased the right to keep her distance from anyone who might have unnerved, irritated, or upset her'. As Hochschild observes: 'Unwittingly, Norma had outsourced sympathy itself.'

The shock of recognition was instant. Remembering my mother's heart-stopping 'What do you even do?' I realised that her world had not only become small it had become mean. What is more I was partly responsible for her inward turn.

By constantly protecting my mother from unpleasant

encounters with members of the wider family, domestic workers, building contractors, doctors and shop assistants I was doing her a disservice. Inadvertently I'd aided her withdrawal from human relationships and stifled her opportunities for expressing sympathy. The cruelty of it is that the more cut off she feels, the more her certainty and confidence are in question, the closer she comes to closing entirely the vault where intimacy lives and loves.

The other day I tried a new tactic. I arrived at her house full of the bustle of my life. I had decided to tell her the truth about my hopes and desires, the things I usually take care to efface around her. I told my mother that I'd been thinking hard about what lay around the corner. That G and I were eager to begin a new chapter of our lives. Now that our child was heading to university we were considering a move to the country. I told her that I might apply for a fellowship in Paris, that I wanted to travel more, that I dreamt of improving my Spanish. Who knows, I told her, throwing tact to the wind, but perhaps I only had 20-odd good years left to enjoy and if that were the case I wanted to live them to the full.

My mother looked at me impassively. Then she opened up to me in turn. She said: 'You know, the fact is that I have no real desire to live any longer'.

I'd been well and truly snookered. Intimacy had returned to our relationship, but not in the way I had hoped. I didn't know if she was trying to tell me without telling me that she wouldn't be around all that long to hinder my plans and that I should therefore consider myself free. Or if my energy simply exhausted her to the point of forcing her to admit that her own energy stores were so depleted she was effectively running on fumes. Or was there something else?

As I left her house that evening to return to my life I could feel the drag of her expectations more not less than usual and it dawned on me that my mother had trumped my announcement with her own stark reveal. It was the ultimate guilt trip: it was me who had sapped her desire to live.

I will not be derailed. I am derailed.

Safeguarding

It starts like this. His ears prick up. He wags his tail and paws my leg, steps forwards impatiently and then back again, as if he knows he's importuning me. If he's acting up bold, he huffs. I feel his eyes bore into me. He has me in his sights.

But I have his measure. My hands are acquainted with every contour of this dog's little body, every crevice and hidden place, as if I carried a 3D model of him in my head, like those computer-generated schematics that spin slowly round in space, a neon outline against the black, calibrating and updating the way his limbs and head are angled, anticipating the force of his spring and bounce.

I wonder sometimes if this is a kind of sculptural knowledge, akin to the way artists see potential for form in a hunk of rock. Or perhaps it resembles the way tactility can infuse vision, a quality that one scholar I've read calls 'fingery eyes', a quality that lets us see snowflakes as fluffy, fallen leaves as crisp or dry. Whatever kind of knowing this is — a lived knowing, time-worn, love-worn — it lets me grasp the dog's wholeness.

Come and see him. He is every shade of gold. Copper-tipped at the ends of his ears and tail, yellow-gold along his flanks, interspersed with spare undertones of black, left over from his puppyhood. Along his belly he shades to champagne. His hair is soft with body oils. It is thick-piled and lush to the touch. Usually it smells a bit rice-y, fragrant with dried-up wee.

I like to run my hands through his pelt, feeling the dog's animal heat, concentrated in his compact body like something motive: an electricity generator powering up in the dark.

Every day it starts the same way. He paws me, implores me and I give in. As soon as I stand he darts to the front door, noses his harness then looks back at me as if to say *What are you waiting for?* There's a moment that melts my heart every time: how he lifts his leg into the harness instinctively, helping me along, making things easy.

And then we're off, hurtling headlong into the urban jungle amid moving cars, pedestrians, a local green where the presence of other dogs drives mine insane. He likes a brisk trot, but in truth it is all stop-start with him. Stopping, sniffing, snaffling, grubbing, panting, straining, scanning. At the first brace of cold the fur along his back bristles up and stands on end. He wants this adventure.

Lately I have noticed that when I am out walking with him a changeling alteration pervades me. It's not marked enough that anyone would notice. But I am not myself, or I am another self, or myself splits. I cannot tell if this canine pull is chemical or material, psychic or cellular, but should another human stray into our path instantly I side with the dog. Something visceral asserts itself — an animal suspicion, the triggered riggings of a primal defence system — and my skin prickles and tightens. A soundscape of singsong chirpings and dull city rumbles fills my head and my vision is super-focused. I am on my guard.

As we walk I start to sniff things out. I detect wet leaves and rot, humus and petrichor. I transgress my own boundaries. Overflow. Should anyone cross me I'm liable to snarl.

The dog has primed me to think with sound, smells and skin, to swab for mood shifts in the atmosphere as I breathe in and out. In tune our bodies move together, sensing which corner to turn and which way to lean, the leash in my hand a balletic ribbon, our dance an agile duet.

Upon seeing a squirrel, time is held to a split second's standstill. The squirrel freezes on the pavement, paws extended, ready to run, its dancing eyes stilled to a laser-lock. But then the dog breaks the spell, bounding forwards in great lunges, his little legs, straining at the harness, pedalling only air. I am seized by the dog's excitement, overwhelmed by an impulse to let go of the lead so that he can give chase. I shock myself with this proxy bloodlust, my enjoyment of the squirrel's fright, my blunt animal hunger. I am gunning for him!

When we spy a fox flaming through the darkness we both run at it, quickening pace together as it gallops off even faster into the night then disappears between the railings that border the green, now submerged in deep shadow.

Back home I need space to recover so the swirl of sights and smells can diffuse and I can come down from a nervy, vigilant high. I have to blink to stop the table in the hall and the stairs rising beyond it from pulsing. For a while my limbs feel sprung. I go about tasks that call for activity as if I need to shake something off.

These days I no longer know who is leading whom. The question is raw and open. But I do know the dog has reshaped me, infiltrated my barriers and turned me inside out. He has my measure it would seem, even as I lose sight of it myself.

Although he has a name I will simply call him 'the dog'. I want to resist cute. I want to push aside thoughts of his beseeching eyes and floppy silken ears or the way with chin resting on the floor he sometimes comports his body to form a line. Looks are deceiving and, though domesticated, this dog is not tame. As soon as we enter the danger zone that is the street — a place that may be crossed only by placing his body on the line — his feral skills come alive.

The dog is insensible to the boundaries represented by curbs, crossings or fences. The city's teeming pavements, bad air and occluded skies pass him by. Only the natural environment springs to vivid action, brittle and buzzing. As I cede to the dog's animal authority I too am learning to overlook the man-made aspects of the landscape. Under his olfactory lead it is the ground that rises up to meet me when I walk him, its newly magnified features as clearly defined as pebbles glimpsed at the bottom of a brook.

This kind of empathetic identification is a far cry from the reserve, even mistrust, with which I regarded the dog when he first entered our lives. I didn't know how to hold him, feed him, wash him or play with him. It was pitiable. Especially since our then 11-year-old child seemed instinctively to know what the puppy needed. Watching them together I witnessed an unselfconscious love, but I couldn't find a way in. Couldn't even work out in what way this dark hairy fluffball qualified as a dog since it was impossible to discern eyes, legs or indeed a face amid the profusion of fur. Perplexed, I'd watch him running around indoors, close to the ground, tracing seemingly random and vaguely elliptical pathways, as if pulled by string.

Left to my own devices we would never have ended up together. But he was the lone survivor of a litter birthed by one of our neighbour's dogs: all the other puppies had somehow failed to draw milk from their mother's teat and had swiftly starved to death, leaving our neighbours distraught. Unable to bring themselves to sell the only living puppy, they made a generous gift of him to our child, who'd been in constant attendance during the whole unhappy drama. There was something about this dog's gritty determination to live that moved me.

When it came to us living together it was the dog who dictated terms. The decisive moment arrived one warm spring afternoon when we were weeding the garden and the dog was cavorting nearby, doing its aimless running-around thing. On spotting a slow-moving, and very likely poisoned, mouse, he snapped to and pounced, snatching the mouse up into his mouth and gobbling it down whole in a few swift gulps. It happened so fast that all I registered was the mouse's muscular tail thrashing wildly around before it vanished into the dog's maw like a piece of sucked-up spaghetti.

From that point on I surveyed the dog with a new respect. I thought: you are you and I am me and we will always be radically different beings. Living with each other will require negotiation. There will be compromises and occasional grandstanding; give and take, push and pull. And I have continued thus, mindful of the dog's profound otherness.

Yet his spirit has touched me in spite of myself. I feel an affinity for him that has allowed us to commune, dissolving species-specific barriers and twinning us in ways I never could have foreseen.

Inside the house that is now our collective space, the dog stakes his ground just as the human inhabitants do. He expresses preferences as to whom he spends time with, which room he hangs out in and he signals his hunger or desire for play or affection with a gruff economy. These silent negotiations around space-sharing have become largely normalised. But every now and then I am struck anew by his *Thou-ness* — to borrow the theologian Martin Buber's term for describing an implicit feeling for the other. I am pulled up by his distinct and inscrutable selfhood.

The dog is a world unto himself. Often he is sphinx-like, gnomic, as though he embodied the mysteries of the ages. 'He is an evolved being', G tells me and perhaps he's right. Frequently we puzzle over how this animal can spend such long stretches of time lying on the floor, paws extended frontward, head raised, statue-still. Laughingly we call him Ra or The Sun Dog. Gazing out at nothing he is enviably self-contained, like some ancient guardian of the secrets of kings.

In the title essay of his anti-humanist collection *The Silence of Animals* (2013) the philosopher and cultural provocateur John Gray ponders this peculiarly animal stillness, contrasting the way animals enjoy silence as their 'birthright' with how humans are forced to seek out silence as 'an escape from inner commotion'. Gray wants to demolish human self-regard. Our yearning for silence is for him an expression of our longing for redemption from ourselves and so we envy the way non-human animals inhabit silence as 'a natural state of rest', or perhaps it is even grace — since animals do not need redeeming. Gray says that if the lack of language among animals may be understood as a kind of poverty, then this poverty nevertheless represents an ideal that humans, stuck inside language, will never attain. Struggle as we might we are trapped by words.

Not long ago we took the dog with us on a visit to the windswept dunes of Camber Sands on England's south coast. We let him off the leash, something we never do in the city, thinking he'd relish the freedom to roam. In our eagerness to reach the sea G and I and our teenager scrambled up grassy dunes and down the other side onto the long expanse of pale sands, from where we ran to the water's edge to get our feet wet. We picked up seaweeds and shells. Starfished into powerful winds to feel the strange weightlessness of suspension, each of us in our own happy world. Meanwhile the dog was running hapless circles around us, sprinting frantically from one to the next, panting and wild-eyed — signs we mistook for excitement. When we got back to our B&B, he collapsed into his basket, not to emerge until the next day. We had exhausted him.

Only later did understanding dawn. The dog had been trying and failing to herd us. Once exposed to the elements, out and about in 'the wild', we were no longer his guardians but his charges. The trouble was we had moved in all directions at once, unpredictable and beyond controlling. Not only was the dog agitated because the task of herding us was beyond him but, given the way he's wired, there was nothing else he could do. It's almost as if at some level he realised that, with his tiny legs, he was not really up to safeguarding us. And then what use would he be?

I often think back to that moment on the beach. I see myself all too clearly in the dog. In my own frantic attempts to safeguard those I love I run myself into the ground. Against all reason and experience I try to cover all the fronts, leaving no one out, and I handicap myself in the trying; I practise a form of emotional bet-spreading in which the gains can only ever be small, while the losses are all my own.

At such times I am more like my mother than I ever thought I'd be, construing self-denial as a virtue, mistaking self-abasement for humility. As if all the crazy plate-spinning might be commendable for serving some unspecified higher goal.

I wonder what John Gray would make of this kind of animal purposefulness, instinctive and deeply driven? Whether he'd raise it up as something inherent and majestic like the 'birthright' that is animal silence?

I happen to think that animal purpose is intentional,

but not the product of higher consciousness — with its fretful headwinds churning up self-doubt — so much as a simple and sensual goal-directed awareness; and if that involves a sacrifice of selfhood, or of pride, then so be it.

The dog herds. I herd. No reflection is involved because it is the old program that is doing the talking.

I am on more intimate terms with the dog than with any human I know or have ever known. Saying this feels as if I'm breaking a taboo. But my clothing is suffused with his smell as with a lover's scent.

We're sitting face to face now, me on the sofa and him on a raised swivel chair whose base I hold steady between my knees. In half an hour I will feel the strain in my calf muscles and arched feet, but for the moment I focus on the task ahead. I calm him, running my hand over his sleek head and down his back, stroking his twitching, leaf-shaped ears. He knows what he is here for and he is not pleased. But I need my hands to rehearse the feel of him and remember again that I can pin both ears back with one hand, tilting his head upwards to hold it still, and that I need to lift and bend each leg gently to access the soft padding of his paws without causing his joints to click.

Although this is a bimonthly routine, every time I groom the dog my heart is in my mouth. What if the scissors (round-ended but sharp) should slip? What if I accidently nick the paper-thin skin at the top of his legs where it folds into the soft pink of his belly? The dog belongs to a species that doesn't shed, so his hair just grows uncontrollably. Around his eyes his fur gets gummed up with eye goo, the hard clumpy spikes giving him what I think of as sniper vision. To delay going at him with the scissors I massage the delicate eye area with cottonwool pads soaked in warm water. Yet within days the sniper vision is back, amid more overgrowth. Long hairs sprout between his paw pads. His toenails curl with excess keratin. Crusty bits of faeces catch in the scraggly fur under his tail. I hate to cut his hair, but I have to.

G teases me, saying dog grooming is fast becoming my side hustle. However, he knows that grooming the dog is an act of love. Perhaps a little part of him is jealous? This work is delicate. The dog and I need to be alone.

I feel an almost unbearable tenderness towards the dog when he submits to this ordeal. I want to meet his trust with respect. I am careful and slow in all my actions. Especially when using scissors, which have to be angled flat against his cheeks to get the hairs around his eyes, then very steep to snip the fur round his nose. On the underside of his feet I've discovered something like a magic button that when pressed causes his paw pads to separate, giving me ready access to the wayward growth.

The scissor ends tickle him and reflexively he retracts his paw. Start again, be patient, breathe. At the end of this process I have a pile of dog hair beside me heaped into a small pyramid. I swivel the dog around to lift his tail and snip the hairs around his anus. His pale-pink sphincter twitches as I work.

Was I ever to inadvertently hurt him the dog would yelp in pain and yet, being a dog, he would never hold it against me. In fact even if I mistreated him he would acquiesce to my will over and again: he would bear everything.

But then there are times when he bears nothing, when the weight of his existence is as nothing. People are forever carrying the freight of their burdens, but for the dog there is no such load, and so the flip side of the dog's absolute dependence is his indiscriminate affection. No matter how much love he showers upon us, for example — his intimates — I know full well that if a stranger walked through the door he would without hesitation offer them the same unquestioning devotion. It irks me, though I cannot tell if my irritation is on his account: how can he be so trusting? — or my own: the bald-faced betrayal of it. My dog is no Hachikō, the Japanese Akita so attached to his late owner that it awaited his return daily, meeting his commuter train at Tokyo's Shibuya station for nine long years.

A foolish dog with his foolish abundance of love, my dog taps into but cannot resolve an inner contradiction within me: namely that I believe love ought to be conditional and yet all too often I do not string cordons around my heart either. I allow others to traduce my boundaries and make myself abject when I ought to be strong. There are perhaps two kinds of vulnerability: one that is contemptible because it does not respect itself; the other that combines self-respect with being utterly known.

I aspire to the latter kind, but I am more familiar with the former.

1

What do we owe the non-human world?
In a recent collection of fiery essays the
poet Rebecca Tamás argues that we
should meet its indifference with love and
extend a generous welcome even to things
that disgust us. In other words what is
required is less a debt repaid than a bonded
investment. We must put something of
ourselves into it.

Ecological thinkers like to point out that
our DNA is roughly only ten per cent
human. The rest is microbial — bacterial,
fungal, viral and archaeal. As the scholar

Joshua Trey Barnett puts it: 'At a very basic level, the "I" is already a "We"'. Which puts paid to a relationship with the living world that is defined by distance. One that relies on dominion, say, or stewardship.

2

But why draw a line at the things which are alive? In *Being Ecological* (2018) Timothy Morton makes the case for the non-living as well. He writes of Danish artist Olafur Eliasson's 2015 sculpture *Ice Watch*, an installation of 12 gigantic blocks of Arctic ice transplanted from Greenland to sit in circular formation outside the Panthéon in Paris — an ice dial, waiting for the sun's rays to melt it. It was a neat way to confront delegates attending the COP 21 summit with a symbolic countdown to our ecological fate.

But, says Morton, the sculpture was so much more than that on account of the way humans interacted with it. How they ran around and hugged the ice blocks and climbed in and out of holes and nooks created by its melt. How water pooled at their feet and created instant splash pools, impressing its coldness into the paving stones beneath.

Writing of the magic and mystery of these interactions Morton's own language breaks down as if it were melting alongside the ice, dissolving the boundaries between mind and inarticulate experience. 'The ice is a sort of Pandora's box with an infinity within it. And so am I. It is that mouthfeel again. I'm experiencing the texture of cognitive or emotional or whatever phenomena. I am experiencing *thinkfeel*, or better, since I can't tell whether it's about thinking or feeling but I know it's real and it's happening ...'

Thinkfeel ... Like John Gray's longing to hear something on the far side of language, something 'beyond words', or like the hybrid notion of 'fingery eyes', here is a term that strains to capture that other, furthermore dimension of our interactions with the non-human. It insists that mind cannot be paramount. That ecological and zoological thought is fundamentally embodied.

Archaeologists have uncovered a grave in Eynan, north of Galilee, belonging to a Natufian village and dating from the late Stone Age — roughly 10,000 BCE — that contains the curled-up skeleton of a young woman whose bony hand rests on the smaller skeleton of a puppy curled right next to her. In modern parlance they are spooning. It's a beautiful thing to behold, with its gentle symmetry, one spinal curve homed inside another, tender bones fanning out in patterned form. It is also the earliest archaeological evidence of dog domestication.

The photographic image of this grave moves me the way I feel moved when I pass my teenager's bedroom at night and see the dog snuggled up on the bed, knotted like a pretzel, or else stretched out to maximise contact with the warm physical presence beside him. They've been pseudo-siblings for eight years now: they have history together. The teenager cannot bear it when my thoughts turn maudlin and I express how bereft I will be when the dog dies. Though he has every chance of living another eight years, for the teenager his loss is beyond imagining.

G and I believed that having a dog in the house would be a good thing for an only child, that it would teach them how to care for a creature that needed them more than they needed it. Yet there have been numerous occasions when the tables have been turned and I have been grateful for the dog for providing vital emotional support, above all during those critical adolescent years when our child was having a difficult time of things. Growing up human can be hard, but I'd never appreciated how much love an animal could lavish upon a struggling human soul.

Of course I know there is a terminology for all this give and take. Animal experts talk about domestication being a 'mutual' not a 'commensal' relationship, that is, a relationship that benefits both parties as opposed to just one. I know there are trade-offs involved. Humans use dogs to hunt, forage and shepherd, guard, track and attack, while dogs in their turn benefit from ready access to protection, vital resources and companionship. Even so this language sounds dry to me, too perfunctory and too reductive. It has none of the eloquence of the shared Natufian grave. We are pack animals looking out for our own just as dogs are, but we are also able to exist alongside dogs in hybrid packs. Some people might call this family.

However rationally I try to think about dogs I come up against my reluctance to parse everything they do into the opposing camps of 'dominant' or 'submissive' behaviours. These umbrella terms make obvious normative sense, but I cannot see how they capture the repleteness of a dog's inner world. All the same I recognise dominance well enough. The dog views the entire territory of our local neighbourhood as his kingdom. Strutting along, taking the lead, *he* walks *me*, throwing pert glances left and right, looking for signs of trouble and accelerating towards any intruder, whether squirrel, cat or crow. He pees on absolutely everything. Lamp posts, trees, other people's bins, bicycle wheels. Though he's all bark and no bite, testosterone rules his world. One of his nicknames is Little Man.

I also recognise submission. Inside the house the dog lives by our rules. He knows which chair he's not meant to jump into, what stairs he can and cannot ascend. He covers all the bases of deference, wagging his tail, averting his eyes, hunching his shoulders and lowering his head. When he is disciplined he cowers.

But the official or normative categories of dominant and submissive fail entirely to account for the dog's affective behaviours. For the way he elects to be our teenager's Emotional Support Animal, as proximate as a shadow, attentive to every sigh; or how he seeks to press his body into ours when he senses G or I might be anxious or sad; or expresses joy and relief via an elaborate greeting ritual when we've been absent for the day, welcoming us home with leaps and demi-pirouettes, balancing on his hind legs and waving his front paws in the air, crazy-excited.

I know what the experts say. But the experts need to account for all dogs and I need only account for mine.

A note on canine etiquette.

Call a woman a dog and you insult her. The implication is that she is unattractive, beneath notice, on the lowest rung of the ranks of womanhood.

Call a woman a bitch and you are saying that she is belligerent, hurtful and mean.

But call a man a dog and you compliment him. With a gentle elbowing in the ribs you let him know that he is a scamp or a rogue — especially when it comes to his relations with women. Perhaps you admire him?

In the lexicon of physical intimacy the doggie position is one in which the woman is maximally available, on all fours, arse up, face buried. A symbol of receptivity.

A man who is considered to be a real dog might hook up with a bitch, but he'd never hook up with a woman deemed to be a dog.

Incidentally, I have never heard a woman refer to another woman as a dog.

Most of us are only dimly aware of our animal selves until we meet with extreme conditions: when we're undone by debilitating grief, when chronic pain drowns intentional thought or we experience fear and its slide into fight or flight. Our animal nature asserts itself and we are surprised by its force. Unaccustomed to such altered states we imagine that we are no longer ourselves.

But what if we are more fully ourselves when our animal natures surface?

Civilisation has distanced us from the animal, even if in the eyes of male philosophising women have always remained that much closer to hoof and claw, sinew and pelt. For centuries men have affirmed female affinity to brute matter, using women's inability to escape childbirth and menstruation to keep us a notch lower down in the order of being. Feminism has long struggled with what to do with this animal inheritance. The impulse has been to run from it. To shed the taint. But what if that misses the opportunity to explore a fruitful tension between our animal and political selves?

In her novel *Bear* (1976) Marian Engel dared to imagine a woman embracing her animal self in its most intimate capacity. On the run from her lonely life as a librarian in a dusty archive in Toronto Engel's anti-heroine accepts a position cataloguing an estate on a solitary island and there undergoes what in today's terms would be called a 'rewilding'. She befriends a bear, eats and swims with him, shits alongside him and then inducts him into an even greater intimacy, taking him as a lover. There is a memorable moment in the story when deep into her entanglement with the bear she catches sight of herself in the mirror and barely recognises the wild-eyed creature staring back, rough skinned and with matted hair: something not displeasing has surfaced.

Rachel Ingalls's *Mrs Caliban* (1982) ventures into similar territory in portraying a depressed and dutiful housewife's torrid affair with a 'six-foot-seven-inch frog-like' sea monster escaped from a research lab. While Ingalls eschews Engel's relative realism and opts for the safer terrain of magic realism (her sea monster is called Larry and he talks) she is bracingly sharp in her scrutiny of gendered suburban mores, her mooncalf serving much the same purpose as Frankenstein's monster, which is to cast humans in deeply unflattering light.

These novels appeared at the peak of second-wave feminism, when sexual freedom had become a byword for Women's Lib — an identification sealed in the public mind by studies like *The Hite Report*, published the same year as *Bear*, and which argued that women could happily achieve orgasm without men and that, in numbers that outstripped previous sociological findings, women dissatisfied in their marriages were active about finding sexual partners elsewhere. Perhaps women were already more in touch with their animal sides than polite society wanted to admit.

But what about when your political self *is* animal? In Marie Darrieussecq's *Pig Tales* (1996) the lead character does not consort with a pig but instead transforms into one, her inner sow manifesting then retreating then manifesting again through the book's pages. At first the woman finds herself subject to sporadic outbursts of piggishness that cause her to eat with greedy abandon, make her skin glow and her breasts 'pneumatic'. Blooming with rude health and unfettered sexuality she enjoys stirring swooning, pheromone-induced reactions wherever she goes. Over the course of the novel, as she becomes more aware and more desirous of this strange takeover (a desire that coincides with a mounting disappointment in her relationships with humans), the sow eventually predominates, until at the novel's end, now 'a sow most of the time', she absconds to the forest and takes up with a 'very handsome, very virile' wild boar.

When I first read *Pig Tales* I was awed by its audacity, the way it made explicit and then amplified the animal part of a woman that resists civilising. But now I see myself everywhere in its pages via the mediating influence of the dog. I see a more creaturely me, who is sometimes agile, spring-limbed, reactive and alert, who sleeps with one eye half-open, ceding to the body's know-how, and who at other times is grubbing and unkempt, who, like Simone de Beauvoir's archetypal bog woman, has an affinity to 'humus … pitch and glue', who is turgid and dozy, lumpen and inert.

Such daring, novelised adventures in animal loving and animal self-expression discomfit us not just by breaking taboos, but by opening a doorway into a terrifyingly egalitarian realm that sets humans and non-humans on an equal footing.

Ecological thinking effects the same destabilising shift. Instead of viewing the chain of being in terms of a vertical ascendency, which has the effect of funnelling our vision through a kind of conceptual borehole, obscuring so much life, ecologically minded philosophers and nature writers picture a place of horizontal extension, defined by relationality: that is, by the privileging of intimate communication with the other over the distancing mechanisms of the gaze. Perhaps human nonsovereignity is something women are especially well placed to embrace, being theoretically, historically and culturally that much closer to whatever is animal already.

Nonsovereignty is a left-field tool. In the hands of eco-activists and academics it is a dynamite stick to be hurled into the midst of every discipline — economics, evolutionary studies, biology, neuroscience, anthropology — to explode the old orthodoxies about who or what is at the top of the heap — developed nations, white people, big business, the able-bodied — and bring into view whatever has been neglected or scorned. It is intellectual anarchy at it thirstiest.

In the hands of feminists nonsovereignty may be weaponised against the patriarchy, which always wants to push things down and be king, drawing a moat around its right to rule. 'These are the kind of fantasies that the nonsovereign bleaches out', says the Australian writer Maria Tumarkin, her sights affixed to clear targets: 'mastery, control, autonomy, certain forms of knowledge, especially forms of knowing *in advance*'. One might add to this: 'hierarchy', or the idea that humans sit on some evolutionary summit. Once you appreciate what the nonsovereign can do, the conceit of sovereignty — its presumption, its blinkeredness — is mind-boggling.

If only we could *thinkfeel* our way along alternative developmental pathways. Rather than trace a line from a nutrient-rich soup via single-cell organisms into ever more complex phyla we could bind ourselves instead into different genealogies, perhaps beginning with *anima*. Anima is the Latin word for soul, the root from which we get animal, animation, animism and unanimous. With anima we might conceive a chain of being that stretches from our animal selves to embrace self and other, motion, spirit and community.

Some days the dog leaps onto my lap when I'm working on the sofa and curls up like a shrimp, snoozing for hours while I am obliged to find ever more twisty ways to type without disturbing him. I stroke him unthinkingly, enjoying the feel of fur against my skin. I sense my heartbeat slowing and my breathing deepen and I believe he does me good. I have come to depend on the quiet harmony of our coexistence and every so often I surprise myself in discovering that I prefer his companionship to the company of other people.

I want to talk about Paula Rego. Because all the time I've been thinking about the way that women's work — caring, cleaning, pleasing, feeding — overstretches and depletes me, making me resentful and polluting my mind with self-recrimination, her 'dog women' paintings have been flickering in the back of my mind. Each of these lush canvases, scratchily worked in pastel, depicts a single woman in a dog-like pose: leg up pissing on a bed frame or prostrate and submissive; on her back with her hands bent like floppy paws. The dog woman is badly behaved and pathetically obedient by turn. One picture shows her crouching on the ground, eyes rolling in her head, her face twisted into a snarl. In another she is spent, slumbering on top of her master's jacket, laid upon the floor like a blanket while a shallow bowl, perhaps containing water, sits beside her.

These works evoke a tumultuous period when Rego herself was emotionally exhausted, washed-out from working to an arduous schedule of painting and exhibiting while caring for her ailing husband, Victor Willing, also a painter, who died in 1988 after years wrangling with multiple sclerosis. It is tempting to imagine how depleting this type of caring must have been for Rego, her limited energies pulled one way then another, her focus shot. Perhaps she felt her creativity was being smothered? Her generosity tinged with a creeping reproach? At the end of a long day she must have been dog tired, worn to the bone. Perhaps she neglected herself, forgetting to eat or to wash? It is easy to imagine how the acid peel of relentless care work might have stripped her down, acquainting her with a not-quite-human self.

Rego invited Lila Nunes to model for these canvases, a woman who was the hired help, taken on originally as the couple's au pair. As Willing grew more incapacitated Nunes began to help him to mix his paints and in his last years she was effectively his nurse. Nunes would go on to become Rego's favoured subject and collaborator. Both women are Portuguese. Physically they bear a striking resemblance to one another and they clearly enjoyed a connection that Rego acknowledged publicly. Nunes for her part prides herself on her powers of endurance (she's said that some of the poses Rego asked her to adopt were difficult to hold for hours), but also on her trustworthiness and reliability — qualities valued in friendship but in domestic workers as well. Perhaps, with the dog women, these lines were blurred.

In the dog-women works Nunes is a stand-in for Rego, an animal alter ego, abject, anguished, yearning, yet sometimes defiant. In an interview with *The White Review* in 2011 Rego said of Nunes: 'She is really myself. I don't like doing self-portraits but she's like a self-portrait. The dog woman was her.'

Describing their working relationship as largely intuitive Rego expanded further: 'She knows exactly what to do, she can read my mind.' From the first time they worked together she gave Nunes minimal direction. 'I just said to her: "Now crouch there, and growl". And she did.' Hastily Rego made a sketch, thinking at first to feature the dog woman as a character in a group portrait. But then she changed her mind and produced the first and fiercest canvas in the series — the one in which, said Rego, 'she's trapped, but she can bite'.

The dog-women portraits make no concession to the male gaze. Rego's subject is inner states of feeling, in the service of which Nunes was unafraid to comport her body as required. The dog women are unvarnished. They are muscular and unkempt, with claw-like hands and hairy toes, a wild glare hinting at a base and dangerous sexuality.

If you could smell them the dog women would smell of pheromones and sweat and blood. They hover on the very border of femininity, a mere step away from the not-quite-human. And they are completely unselfconscious about the way their bodies occupy space. In *Lush*, for example, the subject sleeps propped on cushions stacked against an armchair, head slumped into her chest, her legs falling casually open. It's an extraordinarily intimate pose, soft-edged and vulnerable. The dog-tired woman seems used up, yet she is undiminished by the obedience that is her lot. You look at her and you wonder at how much she has borne.

In a recent catalogue essay Marina Warner notes that while Rego seems to confide in us, 'mining her own experiences', her work categorically resists straightforward autobiography. She does not relate her experiences episodically, but rather 'uses herself as a site of collective memory'. By dealing in types, nourished by myth and folklore, Rego taps hidden reservoirs of feeling into whose depths legions of other women may gaze and see their own inner states reflected.

Whenever I linger over the dog-women works I experience a powerful sense of recognition. Sometimes I am transfigured like she is, a slippage brought on by working like a dog; by the mounting demands of women's work, the caring, cooking, cleaning, washing; and by the sheer energy required to override the old programming for long enough to clear a space in which to think.

There is a tension between subservience and defiance in Rego's dog women that also bristles within most women I know. Women who are constantly undone by acknowledging their nonsovereignty, but who are nonetheless able to find a more layered self-understanding from being so rudely stripped down. At such times the possibility for transcendence can feel as remote as the moon. But then there is a rare kind of exultation in exhaustion, in unravelling to the point of arriving at the very limits of what one is materially capable of doing.

This year we were drawn into a new ecosystem. Noticing takeaway food boxes scattered among the flower beds and deep holes dug in the soil we realised that foxes had made a home along the top of our garden wall, where the ivy grows thick enough to form a tented shelter. Sometimes we'd see them sleeping during the day, flame-coloured balls curled on the outdoor table and slatted wooden chairs.

They drove the dog bananas. He'd fling himself at the glass-paned doors when he saw one, barking and snarling. We had to check for foxes each time we let him out and once outside he'd circle obsessively, sniffing for them. One time we failed to prevent a stand-off and one of the foxes, cornered, took a swipe at the dog. Its sharp claw missed his eyeball by millimetres and a sad trickle of blood fell like a tear.

We tried every benign method to thwart them. Sprayed the garden with water infused with garlic and chilli; tossed human pee onto the flower beds; augmented the flimsy fences connecting us to our neighbours with chicken wire; ordered a sonic deterrent and planted it in the soil like a stake through a vampire's heart. Nothing worked.

Eventually we gave up. The foxes settled in and invited along some fleas. The fleas hopped onto the dog then into our house and began to breed in our floorboards, sofas, carpets and bedding. They bit the dog, leaving him with open sores along his spine. I'd pick fleas off him when I could — a mother gorilla grooming her infant. We went several rounds with toxic sprays and ran endless wash cycles at 60 degrees.

We lost the battle with the foxes. But perhaps we won the peace. After all if I am going to interrogate the human–nonhuman boundary I have to accept the consequences. I have to accommodate the unwanted, exchanging the blinkered comforts of a false hierarchy for the blurring borderlessness of equality.

If I truly love the dog I must suffer the fleas.

And I do love the dog. The small percussive sounds he makes, the soundtrack to our domestic lives, have become as necessary to me as the air I breathe. His sighing, grumbling, huffing and aarf-aarfing accompanies me through my days, punctuated by high-energy shake-outs that can be heard at a room's distance and that sound like *flubba-dubba-dubba-dub*. When the dog stretches himself out like a yogi, head down, pointy paws forwards, his nails curled into the rug, he makes a long, drawn-out scratchy sound, like an old man easing himself out of a chair. It is the sound of effort. When he sleeps he snorfles. Sometimes when he dreams I hear little yelps. At his most chilled he rolls onto his back, leaving his limbs hanging limp in the air. He stares at me. *See what I can do*, he seems to say.

This dog minding is intensely calming. Even when he is folded in on himself in his bed, he emits a faintly perceptible pulsing, an animal heat or mild static, his ears twitch and he sighs a long happy sigh. In my mind I return to the period when my child was small and cot-bound and my sense of their presence was startling and overwhelmingly sensory: aural, olfactory, feral. A time in which I realised that if I only trusted more in my base-level instincts I might just discover that I already knew in my gut, my bones and my skin what it took to take care for a tiny dependent.

Remembering, I look at the dog and I am filled with animal happiness.

Lapsing

Scrolling through Twitter a couple of seasons back a post by the American writer Melissa Febos caught my eye. It was a complaint about unthinking language and the way maleness hides inside it. Specifically Febos vowed to drop the word 'seminal' from her lexicon of praise — because 'why should formative groundbreaking things evoke semen'? After she put out a playful call for female-centred alternatives to 'seminal' I joined the gaggle of respondents who offered a string of high-spirited replies. Because it made me laugh and picture cartoonish ideas budding, ballooning out then floating off like soap bubbles I suggested *boobissimo*. But the coinages that really sang to me contained more poetry: clitoral, oveal, vulvate, luteal, lacteal, hysteral, gynaerous. Here were terms that evoked dark and brooding spaces — undergrowth, grottos, hidden streams, the symbolic unconscious: places where things might be synthesised from organic mulch, becoming impressed with secret shapes before oozing forth from the gloaming. There was something messy and uncontainable about these words, so unlike the perkiness we associate with sprouting seeds.

Febos clearly had politics on her mind. She wanted to protest how maleness is everywhere universalised, not least when encoding creative achievement; how it is the seed not the egg that generates vistas pregnant with possibility; and the seed (or inspiration) that counts even when the most promising ideas need to gestate before they can bloom, or incubate, or marinate in a stew of nutrient-rich fluids. Her post made me think of the way maleness aggrandises itself, arrogates territory to itself and then 'others' the things it discards. It made me think of those early modern theories of reproduction that imagined a microscopic homunculus folded up inside every spermatozoon, the egg conscripted only to provide food and shelter.

Although the crowdsourced feminised alternatives were contrived to make a point, the same way 'herstory' makes a point, they hit my ears just so, setting off a chain of satisfying little tingles all along the neural axis. I have been thinking a lot lately, you see, about the co-dependence of language, body and self, the way each constitutes the other. Where we speak *from* and whom we speak *for* is bound up with our experience — not just as historical beings but as material beings.

The very way I think has changed dramatically ever since having my uterus and ovaries removed a few years ago. At the time I hoped the surgery would free me from paralysing pain in my fibroid-mangled organs, pain that often stopped me in my tracks, causing me to double up, as well as from living with the bleak spectre of ovarian cancer, a disease that has claimed many of the women in my family. And it did. With my organs gone I moved more lightly through the world.

Yet I was wholly unprepared for the shock of sudden menopause, which caused my body to snag up like a choked machine, gears rattling, rivets loosening and popping off, red lights flashing at the controls. One known set of problems had been elbowed aside only to make room for a new and entirely foreign set, more onerous than the problems they had replaced.

I swung into firefighting mode so I might combat the rage, tearfulness, severe depression, insomnia, night sweats, fatigue and memory loss that assailed me. But I failed to see that all the while I was putting out flames sparks were catching elsewhere. Something more nebulous was happening to me, causing my centre of gravity to migrate. I felt as if my sense of self was dissolving, the person I'd always been morphing into who-knows-what.

For months I wandered around feeling queasily off-balance, dumbfounded by having slid from a fluid linguistic modality into an awkward bodily one. A range of interesting speech impediments took hold. Where once I communicated fluently, without giving the mechanism a second thought, I now kept stalling, lapsed and confused. Words flew from my brain and dissipated upwards on the breeze. Nouns in particular kept disappearing. Out and about in my neighbourhood I'd be almost tripping, high on a sense of unreality. I'd speak to people in the course of everyday encounters only to be looked through and unheard. I may as well have been a hologram.

This broken link between word and object mattered. Language is expressive not only of the seemingly free-floating thoughts 'inside' our heads but of our material natures too. When you name things you reacquaint yourself with the world, re-inscribing it daily via a ritual 'hello again'. More important, you constitute who you are to yourself. You affirm that you're the kind of person who notices this or appreciates that, has an affinity for this and an aversion to that, who arrives at an understanding of their particular interiority through calibrating the temperature between inside and out. Noun-mute, I had a hangdog feeling of being locked out of my own mind. The place I was speaking *from* was the void.

Now and again I surprised myself with what did come out of my mouth. I'd say 'pencils' instead of 'flowers', substitute 'wallet' for 'fridge'. If G shot me a look of concern I'd brush it off, joking that my brain appeared to be hung up on morphological resemblances. Yet too often sentences that began well, with clear intention, would lose direction, petering out midway between the starting line and the finish. Too many times, at home, at work, socially, my mouth would open and nothing at all come out. I strained for language without finding it, dredging my brain only to surface dumbstruck. When people looked at me expectantly I'd shrug. I figured this was what dementia must feel like from the inside. But given that bodily trauma is by definition unspeakable I can't help but wonder now if my problems with language weren't masking something else.

In all its varied symptomology menopause put me on intimate terms with what Virginia Woolf called 'the daily drama of the body'. Its histrionics demanded notice. I began to pay closer attention to my bodily experience almost minute by minute, becoming fully absorbed by the proximal knowledge — raw, experiential, strangely insistent — that I gleaned from it. I discovered that with each bodily dip and lurch, each hormonal spike and trough, every shiver and sweat that wrenched my guts, menopause placed a new filter between my reality and that of the larger world. Again Woolf was helpful. Writing about the perspective-shifting properties of illness she described how meaning comes to us 'sensually first, by way of the palate and the nostrils, like some queer odour', twisting our existence around new coordinates, so 'the whole landscape of life lies remote and fair, like the shore seen from a ship far out at sea'.

'Landscape of life', with its connotation of painterly remove, strikes me as just right. It perfectly captures how when ill (or menopausal) we're estranged from the world beyond our sickbed. Turned inwards we have to contend with an immediate reality prone to sudden collapse or rude reconfiguring: once familiar, its shapes, textures and smells (that 'queer odour') grow alien. No wonder Woolf called for a new language — 'more primitive, more sensual, more obscene' — for describing where we speak from when we find ourselves in this altered state. We need, she insisted, to 'speculate thus carnally'.

Woolf's endless struggles with nervous fatigue and what we might now call bipolar disorder are well known. She suffered multiple breakdowns, often following the completion of a book, as if the process of writing it was what kept her sane. The year before she wrote her short essay 'On Being Ill' she'd fallen down in a faint at her sister's house, Charleston. She'd been over-working as usual and though she couldn't admit it to herself she was 'a little used up & riding on a flat tire'. The faint led to many months of illness, debilitating headaches and rest cures. She felt weak then melancholy. She wanted to begin *To the Lighthouse*, saying she had 'a whole novel in my head', but was forbidden by her doctors from writing. Then T. S. Eliot commissioned her to write an essay for *The New Criterion* and 'On Being Ill' (1926) was the piece she submitted. He was less than enthusiastic about it, which naturally sent Woolf into fresh spasms of anxious self-doubt. She worried about her 'wordiness' and the 'feebleness' of her writing.

Woolf's essay bears all the hallmarks of having been written in the heat of the moment and with all the feverish urgency of a patient who wants the particulars of their condition to be better understood. There is constant reference to the body throughout, to its intrusiveness, its insistence on being heard, its animal wants. In illness the body dominates our existence: it is at once tuning fork and transmitter, the principal medium through which experience resonates. Perhaps this explains why, for Woolf, the ill are so lawless. Subject to a body that ails, and yet wants, the ill become rash, wilful and contrary. They spurn sympathy, wallow in sensation. Their critical faculties and good sense desert them and into the vacuum 'other tastes assert themselves; sudden, fitful, intense'.

I came late to Woolf's fiery essay, after having written a book-length account of my own menopause. Instantly I felt seen. Menopause had mainlined my animal self, stripped down my defences and exiled me from my own life; in the weeks following surgery I'd lain immobile on my raft-like bed and surveyed the outlines of the world beyond just as a castaway might. I am not a good patient (like my mother!) and while G and the teenager were princely beyond compare, bringing me extra pillows, toast, books, painkillers and other assorted medications, I found another kind of relief in writing.

In the event, I wrote that book as I lived it — as an embodied woman come into the inheritance of ageing. It was a passion project, full of carnal speculation and distinct from my earlier efforts in nonfiction: cerebral books about subjects that had borne a conspicuous masculinist pedigree. They concerned such seminal topics as apocalyptic cults, the space age and Middle Eastern geopolitics. The minded body — my minded body — didn't get a look in.

My first book about millennial end-times cults, written amid the high-octane anxieties of the fin de siècle, its fear of Armageddon and terror of finitude, was an act of ventriloquism. The words I mouthed in it were not mine but were shaped in the image of 'expert' scholars. In scope and tone the book was crafted to engage a critical-professional class of reader largely made up of men — my unspoken, and unconscious, assumption being that if you write like a man then maybe men will read you.

But I wasn't really writing at all. I was channelling. Much of the time I worked on the project various 'style bibles' sat on my desk, most of them by Gore Vidal, whose orotund, word-clever sentences I sought to emulate, and when it wasn't Vidal I modelled my thinking on Frank Kermode, Oliver Sacks or Richard Holmes, white men with acknowledged status to whose authority I deferred.

Deferring, demurring, apologising, explaining themselves: this is what women do when they intrude on male territory. Did I think these 'intellectual giants' or their successors would beckon me into the fold to share their unremarked privilege? Offer me a matey pat on the back as they pressed forward to open doors? Did I think they might review me or use my book in the classroom? I did not. Yet at some fundamental level I believed that if I cloaked myself in a masculine aura I might get the validation I thought only male readers and critics could confer — a stamp on my passport that acknowledged how well I'd disguised my femaleness.

Proof of concept aside (after all, I'd produced 80,000 words and arranged them into some kind of coherence) there's practically nothing about that book that I'd defend as authentic. I wish to be precise here because the very qualities it aspires to are those I now repudiate in my work. Where to begin? The book pretends to expertise with a brash swagger that today makes me cringe. It aspires to a comprehensiveness that is just lofty generality. And now that I've come to appreciate quietness and ambiguity, often it is just too loud.

To the extent that I've a back catalogue I'm able to lean on I can say now that my first book was a piece of performance art. A strut in literary drag. In projecting a persona that bore no resemblance to my own I pulled off a smoke-and-mirrors trick worthy of Oz-style wizardry: I'd cranked into being a tweedy, bookish, self-satisfied, pseudo-patrician as entitled and unquestioning as a demi-god. If I read closely enough now, trying to hear what lives between the lines of that book, I can catch the wind blowing through empty space — a howl of under-confidence.

To be clear, I do not subscribe to simple binaries that insist 'this is female' and 'this is male'. Never have. But every feminist knows that male cultures and male hegemonies are not in the habit of announcing themselves as male. They just are. They just tell us how the world is. In writing as I did I was colluding with literary hegemony.

I was aware, as Audre Lorde insisted, that, *the master's tools will never dismantle the master's house.* I'd travelled back and forth pondering the merits of an *écriture féminine* and I was innately resistant to the feminist thought police, who if you didn't renounce the patriarchy at every turn accused you of being 'self-hating'. I also had female role models to look towards: Janet Malcolm, Joan Didion, Julia Blackburn, writers who managed to 'pass' without compromising themselves. And still I wrote like a man. It is not that second-wave feminism offered no alternative ways to be or to write, but the options available did not come made-to-measure for every feminist fit. In particular the politics of difference hinged on a relentless separatism that forever dragged women back to the body, enchaining them to it in ways that for me were the opposite of liberating.

It is difficult for me to recapture now my horror of biological essentialism. When politicised at university in

the mid-1980s it was Wollstonecraft's rights-based politics I clutched to my chest, not ancient goddesses, fertility
cults and white witches — those newly recovered shades
of old female power from which I instinctively recoiled
for bringing back to me my ancestral Baghdadi *nanas*,
whose bony grip I imagined extending from beyond
the grave to claim me. I gravitated towards the cerebral,
perhaps because like many children from migrant cultures
I understood brainwork, education, abstraction and
degree-hoarding as a means of self-betterment. I found
'wimmin' whimsical. But I was intimidated by the buzz-
cut lesbians who strode across the campus green, brimming with certainties I could not bring myself to share.

Though I did join a consciousness-raising group,
where I cried each week and railed against my discipli-
narian father, I came under fire among its more militant
members for sleeping with men, being femme and using
tampons, the latter crime slated as just more evidence
of self-hate, since tampons mimicked the penetrative
prerogative of the penis. Others, more self-aware than I,
preferred moon cups. Or so they said. In all its guises the
righteousness of difference feminism felt tyrannical.

Mostly I resented the way any kind of 'feminine' logic
was meant to be anchored in women's flesh, which had
long been used as soil for a flourishing dualism, except
now the values long accorded to the eternal feminine
were flipped. Women were 'naturally' more peaceful,
men aggressive; women listened, while men opined;

women were attuned to instinct and emotion, with men trapped inside cold logic — and where women had long submitted to the male gaze and then shaped themselves into what men wanted to see, now if men cared to look they would see womanhood determined to please itself. *If women ruled the world, they wouldn't have made such a hash of things.* This was the anti-war cry of the day, heard everywhere. And so it went. I can't have been the only feminist in my generation concealing a distaste for everything Greenham Common.

Nor can I have been alone in my dislike of the high-flown French feminist philosophy that situated female subjectivity in the groin. With my troublesome gynaecology, problematic even in youth, I sought escape in the bloodless immateriality of pure (male-colonised) Mind. I had no time for theorists such as Luce Irigaray, who seemed to think it was a good thing if a woman's voice, her thinking, her female *jouissance*, was essentially vaginal: 'Is her end in her beginning?' asked Irigaray in *Speculum of the Other Woman* (1974), here as elsewhere picturing a female subjectivity that perpetually revolves around itself, its edges never-ending, lips always touching, and at its centre a nothing.

It is not uncommon these days to hear women castigate themselves for internalising male judgement. So many of us have allowed male judgement figures of one kind or another to enthrone themselves inside our heads. But running counter to these inner critics I have also got a righteous second-wave feminist kicking ass inside my head, perpetually telling me to do better. She doesn't shave or even wash much: she's not a pleaser. She slobs around the house in her dressing gown for much of the day, grazes at the fridge door, neglects her family's needs, her mothering duties *and* her daughterly duties, and justifies all of it in the cause of furthering women's interests. This is the feminist who wins the day when I am writing, and I don't always like her. But after a long time of being quiet while the miniature judges strutted about tut-tutting at my failings, these days she is increasingly being heard.

The second-waver inside my head was a lot less vocal back in the days when I was man-aping, though I never stopped identifying as a feminist, even in those years on either side of the new century's dawn, when feminism was regarded as an artefact of the 1970s, quaint as hotpants or glitter-framed specs. To say nothing of 'girl power', which struck me as little more than a marketing ploy. But I'm thankful that my sweaty, snarly, stompy avatar was ready to bring me back to myself when I was lost. Emptied out and rendered speechless by menopause, she reminded me that I could not, after all, escape biology. Even if it was not exactly a female biology I was now reckoning with, but a non-biology or a mirror-image biology that substituted a set of curious absences for the politically, oftentimes physically, bothersome presence of femaleness.

It bears repeating that if ageing brought with it an unexpected inheritance of undreamed of and unwanted experiences — which with only the old masculinist repertoire to hand I had no language to frame — it also placed me beyond reproductive life, if not in fact beyond the body. After my surgery I was now on nodding terms with the barren woman, the bitter woman, the empty vessel, the widow and the crone, all of them converging upon an archetype almost as repugnant to feminists as to anyone else: the spent woman, the woman whose purpose is no longer evident, whose value has expired. She is (I am) the stony ground on which nothing ever grows. In fact you can scatter any amount of seed upon this ground and nothing seminal will ever take root.

What kind of subjectivity dwells in this desert terrain?

I hadn't a clue. But I hadn't a choice either. I realised that if I was going to give testimony of menopause then I would have to write from inside this altered state, rerouting my thinking via a body-consciousness that had gone rogue. Instead of papering over my crisis of the self I would write directly into it, sticking fast with that feeling of being unmoored. In writing my field-notes I would be an outsider looking within, an ingénue delivering dispatches from the internal front line, an anthropological and existential voyager.

But there were still things I had to learn. In venturing

forth like a querent I would come to cherish not-knowing over knowing, to value answering every question with another question. I wanted to 'live the questions' just as Rilke instructed the young poet who had sought his advice on writing to do: perhaps one day, wrote Rilke, you might 'live your way into the answers'.

One thing was clear: in my traumatised state of lack — hormonal lack, the absence of a reproductive identity, the profoundly alienating experience of sleep deprivation — I could no longer write in the male voice I had earlier ventriloquised, with its unitary, forward-pointing, linear intent. It was too assertive to dwell inside the gaps of broken language and explore the silences therein or brave the void and bring absence into presence.

Instead I discovered that just as it is possible to feel enlarged by giving things away you can build confidence, in writerly terms, by being humble. I don't mean false modesty or hedging everything you say with 'possiblys'. I mean actually revelling in not knowing. I mean interrupting yourself, entertaining contrariness, letting your thoughts wander then circle back upon themselves, trail off and fragment. When, finally, I let it all hang out, put it all on the page, it was a liberation.

And that went for the body too in all its menopausal complexity.

Like Woolf I had been forced to acknowledge that at every turn 'the body intervenes'. It importunes us, blindsides us, pleads with us, pleasures, pains, arouses and depresses us, sways our judgement and shapes our sense of self. Which is to say our bodily self-consciousness has a hand in forming our subjectivity. Writers can heed it or not and I find I'm increasingly drawn to those who do — Adrienne Rich, Maggie Nelson, Carmen Maria Machado and many others. The point is that in pain or grief, love, rage or illness, in hormonal extremes or sleepless desperation, the body is a window onto the world that changes what we see by virtue of shifting how we see it.

Audre Lorde, so passionate about and precise in using language, so committed to its world-creating potential, celebrated the notion of *feeling* our way into knowledge rather than thinking ourselves into it. She understood that the body *knows* and that this knowing, calling on skin and gut and nerves, ears, eyes and tongue, is individual and particular, not categorically gendered. I like to think of this knowing as a 'somatic sensibility' and these days I actively cultivate it, carving out a place for writing that jars, disrupts and disorientates, and gifts us a sensory idiom that's 'more primitive, more sensual, more obscene', just as Woolf envisaged. The return to the body is my radical feminist turn.

Launching

In the Jewish tradition it is customary to leave a small stone on top of a grave as a sign that you've visited. It's a practice that dates from ancient times when small rocky mounds acted as markers to help grieving relatives identify the burial plots.

These days the meaning is largely symbolic. I always assumed that placing the stone was expressive of a wish to tether someone you'd lost just that bit longer, the way you might weight a piece of paper so it doesn't fly off in the wind. When I thought about the soul I imagined a flimsy, floaty thing that quits the body upon death and drifts skyward like a veil plucked off a magician's casket. But in the mystical Jewish writings of the *Zohar* the human soul is said to be cleaved from the mountain, that is, from 'God, the Rock'. It is literally a chip off the original block.

In the tradition of the *Zohar* the headstone erected

on top of a grave is a stand-in for the soul of the deceased while the stone we leave when we visit symbolises our own soul, now linked to heaven and earth.

Though not in any way religious I am greatly affected by the power of ritual observance. Every January I visit my father's grave and set my stone upon it. We commune for a while, spirit meeting spirit, our encounter a touchstone for the new year. I like to tidy the plot when I'm there, pull up the encroaching weeds, wipe dirt off the unfussy inscription, these simple tasks somehow tapping unresolved feelings I need to purge. I'm always surprised by the violence of these feelings, by the rage and despair and regret that gets churned up as I work, by my own fulminations against the dead and the act of dying, which once released can lay to rest something of my unquiet: the bad juju; the drag of the year just past. I know many people who are consoled in grief by philosophy or religion, but what assuages my feelings of loss — of loved ones, time, youth, certainty, even hope — is more that sense of everything endlessly cycling: human goodness back to dust, Decembers rolling round into Januarys, the baton-passing of generational succession.

There is a plot of earth next to my father's grave that is reserved for my mother so the two of them can lie side by side together for all eternity. This pre-assigned destination seems to remove some of the sting out of her fear of dying, as though it affirmed the existence of a higher order of things that somehow included her in its lofty plans.

But not for me. In my mind there is a clear separation between above-ground and below. I am untroubled by the thought that worms might be crawling through my father's skull, snaking in and out of his eye sockets, or by the knowledge that his flesh has been utterly consumed, leaving nothing but clean bone. These images present themselves to me as part of nature's course. Whereas my mother's plot unsettles me because of the pull it exerts on the living — an invisible force field sucking her in or a horror-movie arm reaching out from the earth. It is an insistent reminder that her time here is limited. An empty plot is a hungry plot.

When my father lay dying in a hospice in north London — a wandering soul many times displaced across continents near and far and now finally at rest — we went to see him as often as we could. We stroked his head with its meagre frosting of white curls and told him that it was okay for him to let go. We told him we'd look after my mother, that there was no earthly thing he need worry about and nothing ahead he need fear. We'd honour his estate. We'd not forget him.

After he began to drift in and out of consciousness he was moved from a bedroom with a view of the garden, where upon his arrival, believing his prospects to be looking up, he'd asked for ice cream and then promptly vomited it up, to an undisguised waiting room, stripped bare of all creature comforts save for a meagre mattress on a trolley. My father lay ramrod straight on this contraption, the sheet covering him tenting over his toes, making him look like some toppled marble statue. His breathing was impossibly shallow while beneath the delicate casing of his sealed eyelids, translucent as lizard skin, you'd see his eyeballs occasionally flit: perhaps the words were going in? Or perhaps not. His face was already a death mask, all the blood drained away.

Most of the time my father spent in hospice he was too weak to talk, but one day he gave G's hand a feeble squeeze, inviting him to draw near, and in a voice thinned now to the barest whisper he spoke. He told G that he wished he'd had more sex.

He did not say with whom, or what kind of sex he'd missed — gay or straight, marital or extra-. I have no idea what prompted this admission and never will. He died on a day I wasn't visiting, taking his secrets with him.

I have tried to write about my father many times without success. I've skirted close, publishing essays about his gambling habit and his final illness, but there are reams of unpublished notes and fragments of writing about his childhood in British Burma and Palestine, his student days in Paris, his lucky and unlucky collisions with history.

Depending on your perspective he had a knack for always being in exactly the right or the wrong place. He witnessed the Irgun bombing of the King David Hotel in Jerusalem from the YMCA next door, getting plastered in the dusty fallout as one half of the building folded in on itself like a collapsing cake. Later he interned at

Maison Dior, stitching toiles in the stewed light of the sloped-ceilinged ateliers that ran along the uppermost floor of Dior's Haussmannian pile on Avenue Montaigne. This was at the very height of the New Look fashion revolution, yet even then the glamorous surface of my father's life was largely illusory. All the time that he resided in Paris he existed at poverty's edge. In order not to starve he sewed lampshades by night and hemmed dresses for his elegant landlady and her society friends, the ever-present threat of having to return to Palestine a failure hanging over him like a sword.

All these abandoned words now lie in a grave of their own.

Perhaps it is so hard to write about my father because people saw in him precisely what they wanted to see. My father had presence, an abundance of natural charm: he drew people into his orbit because he was life-loving and gregarious, hospitable and warm, quick to laugh and equally quick to anger. He made a perpetual show of himself, performing to meet the expectations of whoever happened to be in front of him, yet his essence was somehow ineffable. In seeking to be agreeable to everybody he was true to no one. The mishmash of languages he spoke, his unplaceable accent and pan-Mediterranean looks (he could have been Greek or Spanish or Turkish) only added to the impossibility of pinning him down. My terror has always been that were I to dig beneath all of my father's surface semaphoring I would find nothing there.

Perhaps this is okay. Because in letting go of people you are obliged to come to terms with what you will likely never know. Launching someone from one stage of life into another or from life into death is as much an act of trust as launching a kite or rocket or balloon. You make every preparation possible, then you surrender to elemental forces.

Time and again you offer up your small stone, not as ballast but as an acknowledgement of departure.

Another time, another empty room: this time my teenager's. I walk past it, my heart weighted with what Carol Ann Duffy calls a 'shy sorrow', and I see ghostly iterations of a life glimpsed through its various sapling stages. Standing on fat toddler feet and singing. Endless doodling and drawing. Mugging for the camera in dip-dyed feather boas and gigantoid plastic specs; fixing up superhero costumes from scraps of leftover fabric; journaling in a diary with a heart-shaped lock; strumming a guitar specially strung for left-handers. Painting one wall bright green.

I try to fill the thrumming vacancy that slowly sucks me in by thinking of the many hours spent lolling around listening to music, zoned out in jumbo headphones, all the world's time in the palm of their hand. Of practising dance moves in front of the mirror or knitting that jumper

Harry Styles wore. And the endless train of fads: the Minecraft years! TikTok-ing, Depop-ing, Snapchatting. Snapshotting with the bright-red digital camera, which was a gift for turning 13. All those times they shut the door on me, wanting privacy, giggles and whispers emanating from within. Two teenagers tummy-down on the bed, heads angled together and feet waving lazily in the air; or shut away with a new squeeze, the silence thickening behind closed doors.

If I could string these individual moments end to end I wonder how many months, maybe years this human has spent in or on the bed in this room, in the company of a smartphone or tablet, book or sketch pad. How many sacks of too-small clothing or expired fashion crazes have gone out through that door as shiny new shopping bags moved in. How many weeks were consumed in lying on the floor staring at the ceiling or leaning out of the window with an illicit roll-up. I see 19 years of life run at shutter speed — decades flashing by like seconds.

As for all the months and years of unpaid work it took to raise them, the cooking cleaning and washing; the endless round of ballet classes, music lessons, play dates; the countless visits to the park and library; the succession of colds and fevers to nurse, the slights and upsets to hug away, the nit infestations, exam stresses, crises of confidence and identity: these too disappear into some fast-receding vanishing point when surveyed from the galloping present. I cannot even begin to calculate them.

Besides, time spent such as this is measured in love, not by the rhythms of the calendar or clock.

It has taken G and I some while to accustom ourselves to this new emptiness, to experience in it something other than the tug of loss and to start populating the freed space with schemes and plans. But it is difficult to avoid the mental accounting that envisages one ragged collection of experiences and memories diminishing in stature as another pile accumulates.

I remember long ago a writer friend who has since become very famous telling me that you lose a book for every child. Her delivery was coy, for surely you cannot weigh volumes of printed paper against living bundles of flesh and blood? But her meaning was sincere. She was trying to tell me, ahead of my own induction into parenting, that motherhood insists on impossible trade-offs. At the time I was resolved to keep back something inward-looking for myself as I embarked on motherhood, mindful of how hard I'd had to work in my youth to locate any viable self in the first place. More important, I did not want to model for my child the hollowed-out kind of mothering that my mother modelled for me: two parts self-sacrifice to one part resentment. It felt important to correctly set one's emotional barometer at the outset.

I remember at first how doable the balancing act seemed. At five months old the baby was in the habit of sleeping for two hours at a time in a vibrating chair that sat at my feet while I wrote. What a breeze, I thought, steeling myself against a fall. Surely if I am organised, efficient, determined, then I can make this work: I can earn my living without short-changing my child. Yet before the year was out the full-length project I'd embarked on with the aid of the vibrating chair obliged me to leave the country for a war zone for four weeks, leaving behind at home an infant with a florid case of chickenpox.

The picture looked very different then. I was the bad mother, selfishly putting work before my child (and the bad feminist for anguishing over it). G and I used to say that being away from our child was like travelling without a head wind and on the rare occasions when I was away I rediscovered a true exhilaration in working. And yet my heart was cruelly divided, in that each day I remained far from home also felt like a punishment, the work I'd managed to achieve purchased at too high a cost. As my child grew older I attempted less and less. I certainly lost one book, maybe two or three.

It seems undeniable to me now that the very essence of the affective labour we expend in raising children demands that mothers set aside some cultivation of the self in pursuit of the higher goal of launching someone else — even if the end-goal of all this work is to ultimately make ourselves redundant. Perhaps raising a child is a supreme act of self-abnegation? Or perhaps a piece of priceless freedom might yet be seized on the far side of constraint: that when forced to work with limitations, whether of time, energy, motivation, self-belief or some combination of all of these, your focus is sharper, leaving you better able to utilise whatever tiny window of possibility presents itself. Or maybe it is neither one thing nor the other. Perhaps self-erasure and productivity rub along together quite nicely.

I regularly text the teenager, now living in a city in the North and studying for a degree in songwriting.

What are you doing tonight? ☺
Did you find that Ramen place?
Really ¯_(ツ)_/¯ you wish you'd studied Jazz instead … ♪♫
I'm so glad you had a great visit with [Lina/Lupa/Lexi/Lotte]
I know you miss home, lovey, we miss you too! ♥♥♥
I'll send over a pic of the dog in a mo. He's doing his *have you ever seen anything so cute* face :))
WHAT TIME WAS THAT YOU GOT IN??????
Baby it's cold outside ♫ — next time yr home don't forget to pick up the Carhartt jacket. Brrrrr.
First boil the lentils for half an hour then test to check they're done. Only add dressing when cooled. Xxx
Ahahaha.

The phone is my symbolic stone. A winged messenger between generations, a digital communing, soul to soul.

The empty nest is cold this season: we turned the radiator off so as not to be wanton with heat. Still I cannot pass the teenager's bedroom without opening the door and poking my head in. Just to sniff the air. Just for a gulp of fading teen spirit. I notice a row of Blu Tack spots along the bright-green wall, along which postcards of mushrooms and cephalopods once stuck. Now they adorn the walls of a student flat in the North. The smell of used bedclothes and unwashed hair has dissipated. The parted curtains look forlorn.

Loving well involves letting go. I know this and fight my instinct to cling.

On the eve of their departure for the North the teenager and I shopped at IKEA, clutching a list of items necessary to the establishment of independent living. A vegetable peeler, a corkscrew, a large mixing bowl, wooden spoons, a shower mat, a toothbrush holder, a soap dish, a duvet cover and throw, a rug, a couple of cushions to scatter, a plant (one real, the other fake, just in case), coffee mugs, plates, cutlery: a starter kit for life-building. We wander round together debating the merits of this or that item, whether to get basic wares or top of the range, neutral colours or brights. The brights, we agree, are slightly off, too paintbox bold, a statement but without conviction. We wheel our metal trolley from display room to display room, marvelling at marketing environments rigged up to resemble homes.

The thought crosses my mind that in other societies launching a child into the world of adulthood can be a much messier affair, physically arduous or bloody, and I am glad we have the ritual of the IKEA shop.

To love someone is to admit grief.

To cling is to suffer the inevitability of loss.

Attachment and separation are themselves inseparable.

I am reading about attachment theory and I'm learning that loss need not always involve a definitive rupture. There exists such a thing as 'post-loss' — a state of mind and being in which the bonds of connection continue, but in altered form. This strikes me as a good way to think about grieving for the dead. There is nothing to stop you from holding entire dialogues with them in your head. You can revisit them in your memory store, edit your impressions, selecting good over bad.

But a state of post-loss includes links with the living

as well, reshaping the relationship between parent and child, for example, as it moves from uninterrupted connection to a punctuated continuity. As far as the teenager is concerned this on-again, off-again connection depends on what psychoanalysts might term the 'continuing availability ... of the attachment figure'. That's me, the attachment figure — not as fast on my feet as I used to be perhaps, but just as ready to offer nourishment or solidarity. And I can be permanently on hand, there when needed yet helpfully absent when not. It doesn't matter that our separations sometimes occasion a stab of grief, like 'a burning of the heart' as bell hooks puts it in *All About Love*. I still have a role to play. I am in attendance.

These days the teenager boomerangs back into our lives at regular intervals, on breaks from university. Together we have adult conversations about the latest configuration of their friendship group as we try to puzzle out the particular psychological jigsaw pieces that drive or hinder its different members. I notice the self-administered haircuts, and various tattoos acquired on the sly — but thoughtful ones full of autobiographical meaning. Also new routines, such as daily yoga-app sessions and avocado on toast for breakfast. We enjoy an easy come, easy go familiarity now. A jostling of commitments between friends old and new, and with G and I in the mix too.

I enjoy being a bedrock. I think we've built a solid launch pad. All those years constructing support systems and gantries, looking for the best mixture of air and fuel to guarantee a successful take off, the right emotional temperature to create around our child, not too hot (helicoptering) nor too cold (neglectful). Support arms have held this child through the years, stretching up from ground zero and into the skies; not just ours, but a light touch here and there, at well-judged intervals, administered by encouraging teachers, grandparents, friends of ours who've been stellar role models. When the time came all the arms drew back one by one and the teenager flew.

I try not to think too often about my own youthful struggles because even with the telescope reversed so that things look smaller, revisiting past hurts is painful. But they feel relevant here somehow, maybe because the contrast is so stark between my own path into adulthood and the one G and I are trying to lay before our teenager.

When I summon up that period I mostly see an amorphous gloom, shaky outlines bled of painful detail. My abiding memory is of how lost I felt at a time when my peers seemed to be launching themselves into the world like rockets, trailing smoke at their heels, while I foundered or travelled backwards, not knowing how to go about building an adult life. I longed to attain a stable orbit from which I might circle my childhood self from a safe distance — the Iraqi-Jewish girl, stuck in her cultural silo, nurturing nail-bitingly big dreams inside a too-small life.

Even the freedoms I snatched resonated with gloom. Getting out-of-control drunk or out-of-control stoned — spiralling away from being present towards a numb zone. Swearing up and down to my mother that I'd got a ride home from parties or gigs when I'd caught the last tube, mascara smudged all over my eyes, straining to keep awake against the downward pull of alcohol, teetering along the cold, empty pavement in too-big black suede winklepickers — lucky, I thought in more sober moments, to get home unscathed. Though maybe I did want to find out if, as my mother saw it, the world really was out to get me.

I remember how when I still lived at home my mother would rouse herself once I'd crept in, triggered by some kind of maternal motion sensor. She'd pull on her dressing gown, hugging it to herself awkwardly as she questioned me about where I had been and with whom, while I stared her down with an idiot grin on my face, my mouth too gluey from smoking weed to form a plausible response. The escape velocity I mustered on nights such as these was the sort that suddenly gives out without warning, sending its rider into an inelegant nosedive.

It took me until I was almost 30 to find my way back onto a surer path, stringing up wayfinding lights along roads already well lit for so many of my peers.

'How did I produce you?' my mother cried once I had more or less arrived at the alien planet I'd set out for, there to take charge of my own affairs and write off female shame. Secretly I was delighted. It meant that at some fundamental level she no longer recognised me as her daughter, could no longer make out her reflection in my face.

Nowadays I think that I escaped just enough. That any more remove from my origins would have blasted me too far into space and out of any steady orbit. Because the risk you run in going too far is that you can lose sight of where you've come from, and I never wanted that.

It was one thing for my mother not to recognise me. Another not to recognise myself.

In soppier moods I imagine the teenager returning to the street where we live decades from now, fully launched and independent, and pausing to survey our house, with its duck-egg-blue door and top-floor 'hat'— the slanted roof extension we inherited and which gives the house a jaunty air, as though its 'head' were so full of ideas it's exploding, sending tiles of grey slate up into the air. What memories will rush out in greeting? Will the teenager-turned-adult shed a sentimental tear, or smile a forgiving smile? Or a wistful smile? Or the kind of smile that hides a million tiny sorrows? By then our family home will have become a haunted house and I will be among its spectres. Caught up in my reverie I wonder what's in a life — a clutch of treasured moments, carefully held, a legacy of love? What do I want to leave behind me and what might I regret?

In his final weeks my father, immobilised on a

hospital bed in the darkened living room of my childhood home, obsessively circled back over his own time on earth, to the grumblings of a past that kept repeating on him, to a present full of grandchildren he longed to see grown, and a future he believed would unite him with the departed. 'So short!' he kept exclaiming, seeing his life fly by as if it were swishing along a slide rule or fast-forwarding through highlight moments in a video stream; as if, at 87, he'd been cheated out of some necessary mileage — all that time in which he might have had more sex and didn't.

If I've learned anything from the experience of watching him go, wrestling his demons to the end and clinging with bony fingers to the shards of a life wrecked by illness, it is to let go of things deliberately and the sooner the better. I want to shed ballast now so that I might float off without festering grievances. So what if I never live in New York or Tokyo or Madrid? What does it matter if my Arabic skills remain mired in child speak or the technological marvels my teenager takes for granted forever defeat me?

If it is possible to forestall the assault of regret, neutralising it early with a flourish of maturity, it is far harder to avoid self-reproach. The bitter knowledge of wrongdoing is poison. It diffuses through the body's pathways like dye in water, contaminating every cell. I could not leave this life consciably if I believed that I had neglected my duties of care or failed to show kindness and compassion towards people whose lives are enmeshed with mine.

I think back to the working mothers of my childhood friends, the winged creatures who flew like birds, and to my own mother stuck in the mud, and I have no doubt as to which kind was the more present, the more attentive, the one who witnessed more and shared more. But then every child also drinks up the disappointments and limitations and bitterness of the mud-mothers, and I didn't want to inflict my own defeats on my child. I wanted to model freedom even as I recognised that it came with conditions attached; that there would be things I would not get to do, places I would not see, books I'd not write. After all, those very same precluding factors entailed that I learn to adapt my expectations to the realities of my life, to bend my work around it, even towards it, to embrace the friction.

I think back too to the second-wave feminists who critically shaped my thinking, my other mothers, many of whom felt that they couldn't afford to have children if they wanted to remain free. That having children would impede their self-development or that becoming mothers would dent their shield against patriarchy. I don't blame them. In fact I suspect I'd have made the same choice had I been in their shoes and not just for material reasons: not just because economic independence is the first step towards emancipation. But because the quest to live an authentic life was at that time paramount. If you held your feministic politics dear you had to live them.

Now I see that chasing after authenticity is a bit

like scoring a home goal. It is a decoy that gives me pause whenever I see socially progressive movements set authenticity upon a throne. It may well be more honest, and I suspect we'd be happier for it too, if feminism (the movement I know best) gave up on its quest and instead accepted the inevitable mess and chaos of our lives. That way we might cease fighting the chthonic pull, welcome plurality, accept inner conflict. This is how I've come to make sense of my own life. One minute I'm on my hands and knees cleaning the kitchen floor, the next I am wondering why the richer countries of the globe have not yet succeeded in eradicating poverty. Or I'm advocating for equality for all, while simultaneously curtailing my own chances of attaining it. This is life. Specifically it is a woman's life: because the distance needed to travel upwards from the kitchen floor requires the force of contradiction.

When I try to imagine what ghostly words of encouragement I might offer my child's future self, hovering outside the family home, years from now, rocked by goodness knows what time-travelling emotions, I keep returning to the idea of self-acceptance. To the idea that they should not stake their peace of mind on the empty promise of a happy ending. That it is no bad thing to carry the impress of an original wound. That instead of pleasing, one should strive to be heard and understood. That it is as important to possess heart as to brandish intellect. That inspiration is more often than not motivated by complaint and that it is an act of self-care to trade in your burdens for the blissful release of self-forgiveness. I hope the mature adult my teenager will soon become will have the courage to run towards themselves.

Near the end of his life I was fascinated to watch my father interact with my child, his grandchild, who was nine at the time he died. I was curious about which of his traits the added generational distance would draw out or dampen. He was stupidly besotted with my child, indulgent, even awestruck. But every now and then I saw a wild spark of impatience fly, entirely unwarranted in my view. Given a beat or two, or a blast of oxygen, his irritation would have rapidly flared into anger. Used to his ways, I'd see the spark and defuse things. But had my father been younger and the child been me his inability to accommodate the needs of others would have led him to bolt, sending him running off to claim his right to privacy — a right that women, and mothers in particular, find far more problematic to own. That or he would have exploded.

I noticed what was missing too. How all that patriarchal remove rebounded on him, hobbling him when it came to treating his grandchild as anything other than something to marvel at, discipline or indulge. My father saw other people in a binary way, there either to please him or be avoided. Even when it came to his grandchild he could not see before him a human being with autonomous desires — someone to be supported, not programmed.

According to Simone de Beauvoir housekeeping is the worst kind of Sisyphean torture, the labour it consumes endless, repetitious, mind-numbing. No products result from its undertaking and no sooner is it finished than one's work is undone: in her words, 'a continual renunciation is required of the woman whose operations are completed only in their destruction'. In tending to her house and its human dependents Beauvoir believes that a woman risks losing not just herself, she risks losing her mind. In her war against decay she ceases to live.

Somewhat sniffily, Beauvoir acknowledges that some women might find relief from the problem of living in housekeeping — 'as others take to drink'. They develop an 'insanity' for cleaning that distracts them from their own misery. However, a new kind of misery is born when 'the house becomes so neat and clean that one hardly dares live in it'. I wonder which misery is worse. The underlying one, which the woman literally sweeps under her newly vacuumed carpet; or this new misery, life-denying, self-punishing, which eats away at her as she 'wages her furious war against dirt, blaming life itself for the rubbish all living growth entails'?

It is hard to get around Beauvoir's disdain for housekeeping or for the deluded housekeeper who mistakes the means of her labour for ends: who 'wears herself out marking time'. Trapped inside a perpetual present, refusing life itself, her 'years ... lie spread out ahead, grey and identical'.

But what if this perpetual present, full of busywork and unpaid labour, of dirt, decay and inevitable entanglements with others, *is* life itself?

Beauvoir's scalding assessment of housekeeping rests, as she says, on its offering 'no escape from immanence and little affirmation of individuality'. But then immanence is a negative term in Beauvoir's lexicon — her way, according to the feminist philosopher Mary Townsend, of conjuring the 'insistent loud silent presence of things'. For Beauvoir the realm of immanence is fundamentally degenerative, one 'falls back into' it. It denotes 'a degradation of existence'. By dragging us down, enchaining us with endless petty demands, our material lives block the existential freedom that as individuals we strive to attain.

Beauvoir's coloured view pits immanence against transcendence and declares there can be no trafficking between the two.

It precludes us from seeing anything of value in the immersive immediacy offered by dwelling with domesticity.

Today's philosophical fashion for embodied cognition tilts the opposite way entirely, towards embracing materialism and presentism. It suggests that thought itself is rooted in and also inseparable from the very world it describes; insists that our intimate entanglements with people and with things is necessarily generative. Housework, on this reading, is mind-less not because it is vacant, but because it is embodied. It eschews the higher mind. When we wax our floors, plump our freshly laundered pillows and cushions or make our kitchen tiles gleam we are caring for them and because our lives are immersed in these 'things', because we *dwell* with them, in caring for them we are also caring for ourselves and others.

I feel that I must know this deep down, in my bones or in my cells, which is why I fall back on this base-level care of things even when I'd rather spend time caring about life's intangibles — career successes, politics, the unanswerable questions posed by philosophy — or else lose myself reading a book. It is why when I'm suddenly overcome by anxiety in the midst of writing I might suddenly find myself in the kitchen polishing, washing and scrubbing, cleaning out the fridge or improvising at the stove; and why, when I feel the want of care in my life, I might get to work on the bathroom floor with a baby wipe in my hand.

I would be lying if I said that I was unacquainted with the terrible foreboding induced by the prospect of having to set the mundane world to rights, with its mess, its confusion and the nagging and very ordinary needs that bind and constrain us — our true calling to participate in the world of public affairs drowning before the immanence of our daily lives — on and on until death. But turned to face a different light this very anguish is also a challenge or rite of passage, a call to us to find inner resources that might allow us to fully delve into immanence and come out the better on the other side.

Scaled up to symbolic heights it is the anxiety of the creator who has the awesome task of imposing system on chaos, knowing that the order which results, however provisional, is the very thing that makes rest possible.

In her critique of housekeeping Beauvoir makes an exception of cookery, counting it as a skill. She acknowledges that one can find 'enchantment' and 'poetry' in its alchemy. But then she goes and punctures this vision by contending that these pleasures are spoiled by repetition. In having to cook daily, whatever skill the housekeeper possesses is diminished or occluded and only slavery remains. Beauvoir doesn't see that the repetition is the point. Which after all is the lesson Sisyphus learns in rolling his boulder up the hill over and over for all eternity, defying Zeus's punishment of confining him to a living death by finding happiness in the endless doing.

To glide along a newly polished floor, leaving muddy imprints in your wake; to revel in the feel and smell of clean sheets as you begin to despoil them with use; to disturb and ruffle-up a quiet and tidy room with activity, with friendship, music, work and sex: these fleeting pleasures, shimmering with their own ephemerality, is what housekeeping is for. Failure is guaranteed. At the very point of domestic perfection there is wanton, gleeful destruction. The hard-won order is destined not to last and so our never-ceasing housekeeping is not just beginning over: each time it is beginning anew. It contains within it the promise of advancement. Maybe this time you will fail better.

In this sense housework, to me, is like writing, and not only in its dailiness and ephemerality, the constant exercise of doing it. But the sort of work necessary to make a book is the sort of work that looks like nothing. Then when the book is done there's always the nagging feeling that what you've achieved is only ever a shadow version of the ideal creation that exists in your mind: as soon as you receive the proofs you know, to paraphrase Zadie Smith, that the dream has died. In writing as in housekeeping it is an unattainable perfection that one seeks — and because it is unattainable you are placed on an intimate footing with decay and failure and therefore with death.

Now I question how this blunt acknowledgement of mortality sits alongside my feminism. Is the ultimate undertaking of women's work the same existential task as it is for all humans then — to grapple with our end?

That women's work is intimately bound up with impermanence may explain the way we so readily fall back on a feminist politics of self-actualisation because it acts as a buffer against mortality in affirming the self, which is the very thing dissolved in death. Though it may also be the case that a preoccupation with housekeeping, with the rituals of cleaning, feeding, caring and safeguarding, can help defuse our fear of dying by virtue of prefiguring it in the ego death of selflessness.

Then again perhaps the material work of keeping the bodily show on the road — all that dusting, washing, ironing, cooking and listening, hugging and carrying — offers a more immediate, more animal way to engage with that fear than mere intellectualising. I am here, it says. I am exhausted, sweaty and abased, but I am alive.

Thinking about housework and death puts me in mind of a woman I once knew through a book group. An indefatigable Anglo-Indian international aid worker who was always on the move, travelling from one disadvantaged community to the next, from Myanmar to Bali to Nepal, where she worked on grassroots projects aimed at safeguarding human rights. Not until Amira reached her late forties was she finally able to stay still long enough to buy a flat of her own, and commit to place, as it were. The flat was part of a swanky new development near London's Olympic Park. It had sliding glass doors that opened onto a balcony that offered dizzying views over east London. Its kitchen was white and shiny, utterly up to date. Its wood-laminate floors were pristine.

When I commented on how relieved she must feel to have put down roots at long last, she looked at me, aghast. Home ownership was not what she'd expected. Handed the key to her private kingdom Amira had felt the cold hand of death on her shoulder, had realised, too late, that in having amassed all her worldly possessions inside a flawless palace she had created nothing less than a mausoleum. She found it hard to live there, preferred to be on the move, and when she was home she treated it like a hotel. She used the microwave rather than the stove, did her best not to dirty the bathroom. Her sofas may as well have been wrapped in the plastic they arrived in. She treated her home the way certain kinds of men do, especially those who expect women to maintain their homes for them.

She told me that sleeping in her untouched flat was like being buried alive.

At the time I was taken aback, though I understood her drift. To feel fully alive she needed not just heat and motion and their attendant agitations, but the uncertain and precipitous energy that comes with deracination. Working alongside so many people who had urgent material needs far exceeding anything she'd experienced herself generated an everyday chafing that kept her awake, alert to the workings of injustice, palliation and denial. Yet she had lacked a place of rest, somewhere she might be still. And she'd had high hopes of her sparkling new flat becoming that living refuge.

Now I long to tell her that it really could have been, if only she'd mucked about in the kitchen and dirtied the floors, made and unmade and remade the bed, slept in the sheets then washed and ironed them. Immersed herself in immanence. Cared for herself as she cared for distant others. I had not yet learned myself that there is beauty in perishable things and process to futility. Or that housework makes good on these unlikely connections in allowing there to be joy in the destruction of what is flawless.

Admittedly it is far easier to remind myself of that particular kind of joy when a meal I've spent many hours preparing is consumed among friends with candlelight and wine and talk as accompaniments, than when I'm bone-tired after cleaning the kitchen floor.

But these are two sides of the same coin, or the same psyche at any rate. The pleasure of love's labour, I've learned, lies in its annihilation. Destruction is its reward.

I think that knowing this is why I could never be a homemaker, in the modern sense of the word. Because as well as finding joy in perishable things I long to make work that lasts. This is where writing parts ways with housekeeping — and where I happily trade one kind of spiritual anguish for another. This is life. Specifically it is a woman's life.

Acknowledgements

Thank you to Ceridwen Dovey, fire starter, seed planter, agent provocateur. I have fond memories of the two of us sitting together under the awnings of the food tent at the Sydney Writers' Festival in 2019, talking about what we might work on next, prodding each other, speculating, and Ceridwen urging me to look hard at housework. I think I laughed hysterically in response. Not because I found the idea preposterous, but because I already had several secret files on my computer where I'd been stashing away thoughts on just this subject under the title — as a private joke/not-joke — of 'sex work'. After talking with Ceridwen I began to revisit those files and extend them; then when the pandemic confined everyone to their homes it felt as if an examination of life inside the home was needed. I needed it, at any rate.

Thank you to the many friends and colleagues who

put sources my way: Jessica Au, Sally Davies, Josh Cohen, Tobias Jones, Wendy Monkhouse, Christian Jarrett, Nigel Warburton, Jess Rushton; and to 'True Northers' Anna Barker, Heather Dyer, Tina Pepler, Helena Attlee and James McConnachie for the best kind of professional camaraderie and support, especially at the height of the pandemic when we taught online together in various configurations and offered each other morale-boosting thoughts about one another's writing projects.

Joanne Limburg helped me better understand how to structure verse — as did taking a masterclass with Jacob Polley. Alicia Foster and I had long talks about Paula Rego. Will Atkins heard me read the start of 'Cleaning' at Arvon and, along with our students, offered valuable encouragement. And Jaye Kranz commissioned me to write a short piece for a live reading at Melbourne Jewish Book Week, which I later adapted into the opening of my essay 'Safeguarding'. Earlier versions of 'Lapsing' were published in *The Paris Review* and also in Dodo Ink's sparkling essay collection *Trauma* (2021), edited by Sam Mills and Thom Cuell, whom I'd like to thank for giving me permission to expand the essay here.

Brigid Hains, Greg Klerkx and Samantha Ellis were incomparable first readers — uniformly generous and unsparing. I want to thank them with head, heart and everything else for the time and thought they put into reading my manuscript and offering me invaluable feedback. Sarah Braybrooke's editorial input was similarly critical, her prompts and questions opening up ways to add complexity, depth and, occasionally, jokes.

I'd like to thank the team at Scribe for all their work on the book, over many months of pre-production, especially David Golding and Molly Slight. Also Silvia Federici and Anne Boyer for permission to use quotations from their works as epigraphs.

Not least, I'd like to thank Rebecca Carter and Emma Parry for believing in this book from the very start, and in me.

Notes

Cleaning

Martin Heidegger, *What Is Called Thinking?* (1954), translated by Fred D. Wieck and J. Glenn Gray (Harper & Row, New York, 1968), Lecture I, pp. 16–17.

There are many works on the history of domestic service. Start with Lucy Delap, *Knowing Their Place: Domestic Service in Twentieth-Century Britain* (Oxford University Press, Oxford, 2011) and Rachel G. Fuchs, *Gender and Poverty in Nineteenth-Century Europe* (Cambridge University Press, Cambridge, 2005). Among the most enjoyable and thought-provoking books I've come across about the relationship between domestic workers and their female employers is Alison Light's *Mrs Woolf and the Servants: An Intimate History of Domestic Life in*

Bloomsbury (Fig Tree, London, 2007) and Kate Clanchy's autobiographical *Antigona and Me* (Picador, London, 2008).

Andrea Kaston Tange, 'Victorian Hidden Mothers and the Continued Erasure of Mothering', in *Psyche* magazine, 1 December 2021, https://psyche.co/ideas/ victorian-hidden-mothers-and-the-continued-erasure- of-mothering.

Audre Lorde, *A Burst of Light*, originally published by Firebrand Books (New York) and Sheba Feminist Publishers (London, 1988), quotations from p. 131.

Anne Carson, 'Putting Her in Her Place: Woman, Dirt, and Desire', in Froma I. Zeitlin, John J. Winkler and David M. Halperin, eds., *Before Sexuality: The Construction of Erotic Experience in the Ancient Greek World* (Princeton University Press, New Jersey, 1990), pp. 135–70. See also, Anne Carson, 'The Gender of Sound', in *Glass, Irony and God* (New Directions, New York, 1992), pp. 119–42.

Pleasing

Camille Paglia, *Sexual Personae: Art and Decadence from Nefertiti to Emily Dickinson* (Yale University Press, New Haven and London, 1990), quotation from pp. 5–6. The full passage reads: 'What the west represses in its view of nature is the chthonian, which means "of the earth" — but earth's bowels, not its surface. Jane Harrison uses the term for pre-Olympian Greek religion, and I adopt it as a substitute for Dionysian, which has become contaminated with vulgar pleasantries. The Dionysian is no picnic. It is the chthonian realities which Apollo evades, the blind grinding of subterranean force, the long slow suck, the murk and ooze. It is the dehumanizing brutality of biology and geology, the Darwinian waste and bloodshed, the squalor and rot we must block from consciousness to retain our Apollonian integrity as persons.'

Jacqueline Rose, *Women in Dark Times* (Bloomsbury, London, 2014), quotations from the Preface.

Kathleen Jamie, *Surfacing* (Sort Of Books, London, 2019).

Feeding

Charles Taylor, *A Secular Age* (Harvard University Press, Cambridge, Mass., 2007). See pp. 37–42 and 135–7. Quotation from p. 38.

Natalia Ginzburg, 'Worn-out Shoes', in *The Little Virtues* (1962), translated by Dick Davis, with an introduction by Rachel Cusk (Daunt Books, London, 2018), pp. 9–11.

Richard V. Reeves, 'The Respect Deficit', in *Aeon* magazine, 8 August 2018, https://aeon.co/essays/ restoring-respect-is-the-first-step-towards-a-better-society.

Adam Phillips and Barbara Taylor, *On Kindness* (Hamish Hamilton, London, 2009), quoted in Madeleine Bunting, *Labours of Love: The Crisis of Care* (Granta, London, 2020). See also Lauren Berlant, ed., *Compassion: The Culture and Politics of an Emotion* (Routledge, New York and London, 2004).

Alison Gopnik, *Curious Children, Wise Elders: How Intelligence Evolves* (Farrar, Straus and Giroux, New York, forthcoming). A readily available version of her discussion of care can be found in Alison Gopnik, 'Caregiving in Philosophy, Biology and Political Economy', *Dædalus* Vol. 152, Issue 1, Winter 2023.

Moyra Davey, *Index Cards* (Fitzcarraldo Editions, London, 2020).

Caring

Iris Murdoch, *The Sovereignty of Good* (1970), Routledge Classics edition with an introduction by Mary Midgley (Routledge, Milton Keynes, 2014), quotations from p. 82.

Kevin Cronin, *Kenosis: Emptying Self and the Path of Christian Service* (Continuum, London, 1997). See also, John Polkinghorne, ed., *The Work of Love: Creation as Kenosis* (William B. Eerdmans, Grand Rapids, Mich., 2001).

Ivan Illich, *Shadow Work* (University of Cape Town Press, Cape Town, 1980).

Arlie Russell Hochschild, *The Outsourced Self: What Happens When We Pay Others to Live Our Lives for Us* (Henry Holt, New York, 2012). Norma and Rose's story is told in Chapter 10, 'I was invisible to myself'.

Safeguarding

Eva Hayward, 'Fingeryeyes: Impressions of Cup Corals', *Cultural Anthropology* Vol. 25, Issue 4, 2010, pp. 577–99.

John Gray, *The Silence of Animals: On Progress and Other Modern Myths* (Allen Lane, London, 2013), quotations from pp. 162–5. See also Donna J. Haraway, *When Species Meet* (University of Minnesota Press, Minneapolis, 2008).

Rebecca Tamás, *Strangers: Essays on the Human and Nonhuman* (Makina Books, London, 2020).

Joshua Trey Barnett, 'Thinking Ecologically with Judith Butler', *Culture, Theory and Critique* Vol. 59, Issue 1, 2018, pp. 20–39.

Timothy Morton, *Being Ecological* (Pelican Books, London, 2018), pp. 119–31.

For a range of expert writings on dog behaviour, evolution and domestication see the collection of essays in James Serpell, ed., *The Domestic Dog, Its Evolution, Behaviour and Interactions with People* (Cambridge University Press, Cambridge, 2017).

Maria Tumarkin, 'Wildness: Feminism, Identity and the Willingness to be Defeated', *The Yale Review*

Vol. 108, Issue 4, 2020, https://yalereview.org/article/
maria-tumarkin-wildness-feminism-undiminished.

'Interview with Paula Rego', *The White Review*, January
2011, https://www.thewhitereview.org/feature/
interview-with-paula-rego/.

Lila Nunes, interviewed by Rebecca Nicholson,
The Guardian, 3 February 2018, https://www.
theguardian.com/artanddesign/2018/feb/03/
artists-models-paula-rego-lucian-freud-frank-auerbach.

Marina Warner, 'Dream Realism', in Elena Crippa, ed.,
Paula Rego (Tate Publishing, London, 2021), pp. 28–39.
Quotations from p. 31.

Lapsing

Virginia Woolf, *On Being Ill*, with an introduction by
Hermione Lee (Paris Press, Ashfield, Mass., 2002),
quotations from pp. xiv, xviii, 5, 7, 8, 10, 20 and 22.

Luce Irigaray, *Speculum of the Other Woman* (1974),
translated by Gillian Gill (Cornell University Press,
Ithaca, NY, 1985). See pp. 232 and 240. Irigaray talks
again about women's autoerotic subjectivity in her essay
'This Sex Which Is Not One', reprinted in a book of

essays under the same title, translated by Catherine
Porter, with Carolyn Burke (Cornell University Press,
Ithaca, NY, 1985).

Two wonderful essays dealing variously with the
patriarchal hauntings besetting feminist subjectivity
are: Claire Vaye Watkins, 'On Pandering', in *Tin House*
magazine, 23 November 2015, https://tinhouse.com/
on-pandering/. And Olivia Sudjic's *Exposure* (Peninsula
Press, London, 2018).

Rainer Maria Rilke, *Letters to a Young Poet* (1929),
translated and introduced by Mark Harman (Harvard
University Press, Cambridge, Mass., 2011), quotation from
pp. 45–6. Rilke wrote ten tutelary letters to the poet Franz
Kappus, who'd approached the already-famous 28-year-old
Rilke out of the blue in 1902 wanting advice. Kappus's
letters have never been printed, but Rilke's, written between
1902 and 1908, have become iconic. The full passage I
quote reads: 'I should like to ask you, dear sir … to show
patience towards everything in your heart that has not been
resolved and to try and cherish *the questions themselves*, like
sealed rooms and books written in a language that is very
foreign. Do not hunt for the answers just now — they
cannot be given to you because you cannot live them.
What matters is that you live everything. And you must
now *live* the questions. One day perhaps you will gradually
and imperceptibly live your way into the answer.'

Audre Lorde, 'The Master's Tools Will Never Dismantle the Master's House'. This essay has been widely reprinted, including in a collection of essays published under the same title (Penguin, London, 2018).

Launching

Carol Ann Duffy, ed., *Empty Nest: Poems for Families* (Picador, London, 2021).

Jeremy Holmes, 'Termination in Psychoanalytic Psychotherapy: An Attachment Perspective', *European Journal of Psychoanalysis*, https://www.journal-psychoanalysis.eu/termination-in-psychoanalytic-psychotherapy-an-attachment-perspective-2/. See also, Jack Novick, 'Termination Conceivable and Inconceivable', *Psychoanalytic Psychology* Vol. 14, Issue 2, pp. 145–62. And Dennis Klass, Phyllis R. Silverman and Steven Nickman, eds., *Continuing Bonds: New Understandings of Grief* (Taylor & Francis, Washington DC, 1996).

Simone de Beauvoir, *The Second Sex* (1949), translated and edited by H. M. Parshley (Penguin, London, 1987), quotations from chapters 'The Married Woman' and 'The Independent Woman'.

Mary Townsend, 'Housework', *The Hedgehog Review* Vol. 18, Issue 1, Spring 2016, pp. 114–25, https://hedgehogreview.com/issues/work-in-the-precarious-economy/articles/housework. In discussing the care of things I have leant on Townsend's probing discussion of how spiritually challenging is the world of immanence.

Zadie Smith, 'That Crafty Feeling', *Culture.org*, 1 June 2008, https://culture.org/that-crafty-feeling. This is one of the most enjoyable, witty, insightful and honest essays I've read about the experience of writing for publication.